Pre-TOEFL® Guide

Academic English Practice

- Great for IELTS® too! -

by

Bruce Stirling

copyright © 2017 by Bruce Stirling

Editors: the Spring 2017 TOEFL Class, Sacred Heart University, Fairfield CT USA;
Patricia Stirling, Marjan Behbahani, Shahla Morsali

Audio written and produced by Bruce Stirling.

ISBN-10: 1–944595–14–7

ISBN-13: 978–1–944595–14–2

Published by Nova Press

9058 Lloyd Place
Los Angeles, CA USA 90069
1-310-275-3513
info@novapress.net
www.novapress.net

Visit Nova Press at www.LinkedIn.com

Also by Bruce Stirling

TOEFL® Strategies: A Complete Guide to the iBT
Nova Press, Los Angeles USA

Scoring Strategies: A Complete Guide to the TOEFL® iBT
Nova Press, Los Angeles USA

Speaking and Writing Strategies for the TOEFL® iBT
Nova Press, Los Angeles USA

Speaking and Writing Strategies for the TOEFL® iBT
Chinese translation
Foreign Language Teaching and Research Press
Beijing, China

500 Words, Phrases and Idioms for the TOEFL® iBT
plus **Typing Strategies**
Nova Press, Los Angeles USA

Practice Tests for the TOEFL® iBT
Nova Press, Los Angeles USA

TOEFL Strategies: Quick Reference Guide
Amazon.com

Business English: Speaking and Writing Strategies
Amazon.com

Business Idioms in America
Nova Press, Los Angeles USA

Visit Bruce Stirling at www.LinkedIn.com

The audio for this book is available as a free download at:

www.testprepcenter.com/download/

Contents

What is Pre-TOEFL?

Do you plan to take TOEFL or IELTS but are not ready for the challenge? Do you need more practice? If you do, then this book is for you. It is also for those who just want to practice academic English. Whatever your purpose, this book will give you the foundation in academic English you need for TOEFL and IELTS success.

TOEFL Facts

TOEFL means *Test of English as a Foreign Language*. TOEFL is one of the most popular English language proficiency tests in the world. The TOEFL PBT (paper-based test) was the original TOEFL test. It was replaced by the TOEFL CBT (computer-based test), which was replaced by the TOEFL iBT (internet-based test). The three test scores are compared below.

- **REMEMBER**: *On test day, you will take the TOEFL iBT. Since 2005, the year the TOEFL iBT was introduced, the average yearly worldwide TOEFL iBT score for all test-takers has been 81 out of 120.*

TOEFL Score Comparison Chart

TOEFL iBT	TOEFL CBT	TOEFL PBT
120	300	677
110	270	637
100	250	600-603
90	233	577
80	213	550
70	193	523
60	170	497

The TOEFL iBT

The TOEFL iBT is four hours long and has four sections: reading, listening, speaking, and writing. Each section is worth 30 points for a total of 120 points (see *Task Order* next page). TOEFL is designed and administered by New Jersey-based Educational Testing Service (ETS). You must take the test at an official ETS test center. Your responses will be sent by internet to ETS to be scored.

You can take the TOEFL test as often as you wish. Your score is good for two years. You will receive your unofficial score by regular mail within ten business days after the test. For security purposes, ETS will send your official TOEFL score directly to the school/agency of your choosing upon your request. You must pay ETS a fee for each official TOEFL score request.

- **REMEMBER**: *Visit www.ets.org/toefl for more information about the TOEFL iBT.*

Task Order

The TOEFL iBT has four test sections (see below). You may take notes throughout the test.

Section	Task	Questions	Total Time	Score
Reading	3-4 passages	12-14 questions each	60-80 minutes	30/30
Listening	2-3 conversations	5 questions each		
	4-6 lectures	6 questions each	60-90 minutes	30/30
BREAK			10 minutes	
Speaking	independent	2 tasks	2 minutes	
	integrated	4 tasks	18 minutes	30/30
Writing	integrated	1 task	25 minutes	
	independent	1 task	30 minutes	30/30
TOTAL			4 hours	120/120

What does the TOEFL iBT measure?

The TOEFL iBT measures (tests) academic English language proficiency on a scale from 0 to 120. Specifically, TOEFL measures your ability to apply academic English across four skill sets: reading, listening, speaking, and writing. As you can see, TOEFL is really a *Test of __academic__ English as a foreign language.*

TOEFL also measures your ability to learn new topics, then answer questions about them.

Topics → TOEFL is a Teaching Test

The topics TOEFL uses for testing are from first and second year university life sciences and humanities courses, such as biology, art, geology, zoology, and literature. TOEFL does not test applied sciences, such as physics and mathematics, nor does it test current events.

- **REMEMBER:** *You do not need to study life sciences or the humanities before you take the test. On test day, TOEFL will teach you all you need to know to answer the questions. In this way, TOEFL is also a teaching test.*

Can I fail TOEFL?

No. You cannot pass or fail the TOEFL test. TOEFL simply measures your ability to understand and apply academic English on a scale from 0 to 120. The higher your score, the higher your academic English language proficiency.

What TOEFL iBT score do I need?

Undergraduate applicants to U.S. colleges should aim for at least 80/120. U.S. graduate school applicants should aim for at least 90/120.

- **REMEMBER:** *Each school has a different TOEFL requirement. Before you take the test, contact the schools of your choosing and ask for their TOEFL requirements. Professional-license applicants should consult their licensing agencies for their TOEFL requirements.*

How important is TOEFL?

Your TOEFL score, like your IELTS score, is only one part of your college application. You will also be required to write a personal essay, submit your official grades, and provide letters of recommendation. Most U.S. and Canadian schools base admittance on your application as a whole.

What is the SAT?

If you are a non-native, English speaking student applying as an undergraduate in the U.S., you might also have to submit an SAT score. SAT means *Scholastic Aptitude Test*. American high school students take the SAT before graduation. The SAT tests high school reading, writing, and math.

- **REMEMBER:** *Visit www.collegeboard.org for more information about the SAT. Also, contact those schools to which you are applying and ask for their SAT requirements and for any other test requirements.*

How to Register for TOEFL

In the United States, the busiest testing times are at the end of each semester when TOEFL courses end and TOEFL students are ready to take the test. TOEFL is very popular. Seating is limited. Register early. For registration information, visit www.ets.org/toefl.

How to Prepare for TOEFL

There are no fast and easy ways to prepare for TOEFL. There are no shortcuts, no secret strategies. TOEFL, like IELTS, is too long and complex for such simple solutions. Test-takers who get high scores studied long and hard. They took academic ESL classes and TOEFL classes, and practiced, practiced, practiced. They were persistent and diligent, and became test-ready. That is the secret to TOEFL success.

- **REMEMBER:** *Many test-takers can converse proficiently using conversational (informal) English. As a result, they think they are ready for TOEFL. They are not.*

- **WARNING:** *There is no connection between speaking conversational English proficiently and a good TOEFL score. Many students are great at speaking English conversationally, yet they get low TOEFL scores. Why? Because TOEFL tests academic English not conversational English. Academic English is formal English, whereas conversational English is informal.*

- **REMEMBER:** *Being able to speak conversational English proficiently is a good foundation upon which to develop verbal academic English proficiency. That said, remember that the TOEFL speaking section is only 25% of your final score. For the rest of the test, you must apply academic English when reading, listening, and writing. For those tasks, and for TOEFL in general, you need to prepare. The following are suggested ways to prepare for TOEFL.*

Taking a TOEFL Class

Preparing for TOEFL is stressful. You feel like you are climbing a mountain with no end in sight. To reduce stress, I recommend that you take a pre-TOEFL or a TOEFL class. By doing so, you will meet people like yourself. Because you are all climbing the same mountain together, you can support each other by sharing your concerns. This, in turn, will relieve some of the pressure you feel and give you more confidence. Confidence is critical for TOEFL success. It means you are test-ready.

Another benefit of taking a TOEFL class is the instructor. An experienced TOEFL instructor will teach you tips and strategies not found in TOEFL guides. A good instructor will also rate your speaking and writing responses objectively, something you cannot do if you prepare alone. Also, if you are having difficulty understanding a strategy—or don't know why you keep scoring low on practice tests—an instructor will be able to help you. Finally, in a TOEFL class, you will meet people who have taken the TOEFL test. Learn from their experiences. It is invaluable.

- **REMEMBER:** *A good TOEFL instructor has taken the TOEFL iBT. He/she knows what TOEFL pressure feels like. As a result, he/she understands the challenges you face and what you need to do for TOEFL success.*

Self-Study

Preparing for TOEFL by yourself has advantages and disadvantages. An advantage is you save money by not taking a TOEFL class. Also, you are free to set your own study schedule and buy the TOEFL books you prefer. This approach is good for those test-takers who know their weaknesses. For example, Anna knows she needs to improve her reading score. She knows because she took the TOEFL test. She got good scores in listening, speaking, and writing, but her reading score was low. She needs to increase it to get into the school of her choosing. Knowing this, Anna can focus on the reading section on her own. In other words, she knows the problem and the solution. This is called targeted studying.

Self-study is definitely an option, but there are disadvantages. One is, as mentioned, you feel like you are climbing a mountain alone. With no guidance or support, you might feel lost and stop studying. Another drawback is no instructor to offer tips, such as time-management strategies. Moreover, when studying alone, you will be easily distracted. Distractors are family, friends, pets, boredom, and your phone. If you are preparing alone, turn off your phone. Your phone is a major distractor. Preparing for TOEFL takes concentration. Phone messages interrupt your concentration. That said, some test-takers do well studying alone. They have the discipline and the focus. Others need the structure of a classroom. How you prepare for TOEFL is up to you. However, as mentioned, I recommend taking a TOEFL or a pre-TOEFL class no matter what your English level is. TOEFL is long and challenging. The more help you get, the more confident you will be on test day.

- **REMEMBER:** *My TOEFL students prefer to prepare for TOEFL using paper-based books because they can highlight and make notes directly on the pages.*

TOEFL Lessons Online

Many TOEFL websites say, "We can help you pass the TOEFL test!" Sounds great, right? There is only one problem: you cannot pass or fail the TOEFL test. TOEFL simply measures your academic English language proficiency on a scale from 0 to 120. If a website says "We can help you pass the TOEFL test," save your money. If a TOEFL website/instructor does not know that TOEFL is not pass or fail—one of the most fundamental facts about TOEFL—save your money.

How do you find expert online TOEFL instructors? Before you sign up for TOEFL lessons online, ask the online instructor how he/she is different from everybody else, and why? Ask if he/she has taken the TOEFL iBT and what his/her score was. Ask if you can contact his/her customers to get their opinions about the instructor/website. Finally, ask for a free demonstration lesson. Remember: It is your time, your money, and your future.

The Scope of this Book

To succeed at an American college, you must know and be able to apply academic English. Academic English means analyzing and developing arguments. That is what American college students do. They read essays (written arguments), listen to lectures (verbal arguments), give presentations (verbal arguments), and write essays (written arguments). TOEFL, with its four test sections—reading, listening, speaking, and writing—is designed to reflect the American college experience. That means that TOEFL, like U.S. colleges, is all arguments. It also means that if you want to get the TOEFL score you need, you must be able to analyze and develop written and verbal arguments on test day. This book will prepare you for these challenges by teaching you the argument strategies and the academic English you need to build a foundation for TOEFL success.

Part I → *Argument Strategies*

These fundamental strategies will teach you how to argue subjectively and objectively when writing and speaking. You will also learn how to summarize when writing and when speaking. Being able to argue and summarize proficiently is essential for TOEFL and IELTS, and for success at an American university. Each topic in this section is followed by exercises divided into three levels. The levels get more challenging as you work your way through the book.

Part II → *Academic English Practice*

This section consists of three grouped exercises. They are *Structure, Written Expression,* and *Vocabulary*. The questions are all multiple-choice. These exercises are not on the TOEFL test but are excellent academic English practice nonetheless. Combined, they will help you build an academic English vocabulary and introduce you to college-level English grammar as well. These exercises get more challenging as you work your way through the book.

By practicing parts one and two, you will develop the academic English foundation you need for TOEFL and IELTS success, and for college success in the U.S.

- **REMEMBER**: *This book is an introduction to basic academic English essential for TOEFL. It is not a TOEFL preparation guide. For that, see my book TOEFL Strategies: A Complete Guide to the iBT available from NovaPress.net.*

- **REMEMBER**: *Time yourself when doing the exercises. Timing yourself is important for many reasons, including: 1) it will prepare you for the timed exercises in a TOEFL preparation class; 2) it will help you develop automaticity. Automaticity is your ability to answer naturally without translating or hesitating, and; 3) it will prepare you for the TOEFL test.*

- **WARNING:** *Do not take the TOEFL test without preparing. Many have taken the test without preparing only to realize that TOEFL was harder than they had expected. The result was a low score and a waste of money paying for the test.*

<u>Part I</u>

Argument Strategies

What is an Argument?

TOEFL is an academic English test. Academic English means arguments. An argument is an attempt to inform and persuade an audience. A written argument is called an essay. For the TOEFL reading section, you will read three passages. Each passage is an essay. For the listening section, you will listen to three lectures, one discussion, and two conversations. Each is an argument. For the speaking section, you will develop and deliver six short verbal arguments. For the writing section, you will write two responses: a summary of two arguments (one written, one verbal) followed by a personal essay in which you state your opinion and support it with examples. As you can see, TOEFL is indeed all arguments. In order to analyze and develop arguments, you need tools. Those tools are called rhetorical strategies.

Rhetorical Strategies

A carpenter uses a hammer. A hammer is a tool. A baker uses an oven. An oven is a tool. A musician uses a violin. A violin is a tool. When analyzing and developing arguments, speakers and writers also use tools. Those tools are called rhetorical strategies. The following eight rhetorical strategies are essential for understanding and applying academic English and for TOEFL success. Memorize them.

1. *Narration*

Narration describes the passing of time. Note the <u>time words</u> in the samples.

a. <u>Every Monday after</u> work, Phil goes to the gym and practices karate <u>for an hour. When he is finished</u>, he takes the bus to his TOEFL class.

b. <u>Yesterday, Jane got up at seven o'clock</u> and took a shower. <u>After that</u>, she had breakfast, <u>then</u> rode the bus to work. <u>When she got to work</u>, she checked her email, <u>then</u> discussed the new business plan with her colleagues.

2. *Process*

Process means putting events in sequential or <u>step-by-step order</u>. In the examples below, note how each process also describes the passing of time. When describing a process, the step order is very important. Unlike narration, the steps in a process must be in the correct order for the process to occur successfully.

a. When making tea, <u>first</u> boil water. <u>Next</u>, put a tea bag into a cup. <u>When</u> the water is boiling, <u>pour</u> the water into the cup. <u>Finally</u>, add milk and sugar as you prefer.

b. *Titanic* <u>hit</u> an iceberg, <u>broke</u> in two, then <u>sank</u>.

3. _Description_

Description creates pictures of people, places and things using <u>adjectives</u> and <u>adverbs</u>. Description appeals to the senses: smell, sight, taste, hearing, and touch.

a.   Alberto, the <u>guitar player</u> in the band, is wearing a <u>red leather</u> jacket, <u>black leather pants</u> and <u>old motorcycle boots</u>.

b.   <u>The old man lived alone</u> in a <u>really old house</u> <u>high on a rugged cliff</u> overlooking a stormy sea.

4. _Illustration_

Illustration means evidence or _examples_ which develop the <u>topic</u>, for example:

a.   There are many types of <u>hamburgers</u>. For example, there are _cheeseburgers, bacon burgers_, and _veggie burgers_.

b.   When you visit <u>Miami</u>, I suggest you _South Beach_ and _the Everglades_.

5. _Compare-and-Contrast_

Compare-and-contrast describes the _<u>differences</u>_ and _<u>similarities</u>_ between two or more objects, people, or ideas. Compare-and-contrast also describes differences in opinion, for example:

a.   Fatima tried the _pumpkin pie_ and decided the _peach pie_ was sweeter.

b.   _<u>Mary believes</u>_ that all high school students should wear school uniforms; _<u>however, Billy believes</u>_ that students should have the right to choose.

6. _Definition_

A definition is a dictionary-like _description_ of a <u>topic</u>, for example a person, place, object, or an idea.

a.   An <u>argument</u> _is an attempt to inform and persuade an audience._

b.   <u>TOEFL</u> _is an English-language proficiency test developed by ETS._

7. _Classification_

To classify means to put people, things, and ideas into _sub groups_ under a <u>main topic</u>, for example:

a.   There are three kinds of <u>wine</u>: _red, white, and rosé._

b.   _TOEFL, TOEIC, and IELTS_ are all <u>English-language proficiency tests</u>.

8. *Cause-and-Effect*

We use cause-and-effect to describe a **cause** (action) and the *effects* (results) of that action, for example:

a.   **Cora studied hard** *and got a high TOEFL score.*

b.   **Global warming** *is melting the ice at the South Pole.*

Exercise #1: Rhetorical Strategies → Level 1

Task: Identify the rhetorical strategies in the following sentences. Note: A sentence will often have more than one rhetorical strategy. The answers are on page 166.

1.   Bananas are grown in both tropical and sub-tropical zones.

2.   Maria has always been a hard worker unlike her brother who is lazy.

3.   Yesterday was so cold that my car wouldn't start, but my wife's started no problem.

4.   Canada is bigger than the United States but smaller than Russia.

5.   "The early bird gets the worm" is a popular idiom that means hard work will eventually pay off.

6.   After I got home, I made a late dinner, watched TV, then went to bed. I got up at seven a.m., showered, then met my best friend for an early breakfast.

7.   At the organic store, you can buy long grain rice, medium grain, and short grain.

8.   Last year, Al traveled to Japan, Iran, Turkey and Latvia but not Taiwan.

9.   If you want to study in the United States, you must get a student visa.

10. Eva is a shopaholic. She loves to buy French shoes, Italian handbags and American designer jeans. However, she loves buying hats most of all.

11. In China, killing the endangered panda, an animal that eats only bamboo, is punishable by death.

12. Four sitting American presidents have been assassinated: Lincoln (1865), Garfield (1881), McKinley (1901), and Kennedy (1963).

13. An eight-ounce glass of milk has eight grams of protein, whereas a similar glass of almond milk contains one gram of protein.

14. A pro-con debate is an argument in which two or more people support opposing sides of an issue, for example, gun control in America.

15. Coca Cola, the world's most popular soft drink, was invented in 1886. It was originally sold as medicine to increase brain and muscle power.

Exercise #2: Rhetorical Strategies → Level 2

Task: Identify as many rhetorical strategies as you can in the following passages. Check your answers on page 168.

1
2
3
4
5
1. The Emperor penguin is the largest penguin in the world, standing on average 45 inches tall. To survive the harsh Antarctic winters, they huddle together for warmth. This cooperative behavior is unique in the animal world. The female gives birth to one egg, then leaves it behind with the male as she goes off in search of food. Food is in the ocean, often a 30-mile walk from the rookery.

1
2
3
4
5
6
7
8
9
2. Diabetes is one of the most common diseases in the world today. Yet few know who discovered insulin, the drug that helps patients fight diabetes. Insulin was discovered by Canadian doctors Frederick Banting and Charles H. Best in 1921. They extracted insulin from the pancreas of a healthy dog, then injected it into a dog suffering from diabetes. The sick dog recovered. With the help of chemists J.J.R. Macleod and James Collip, they developed human insulin. They tested it on a diabetic boy close to death and he miraculously recovered. In 1923, Best and MacLeod won the Nobel Prize for medicine. However, controversy ensued. Banting believed that Best and Collip were overlooked by the committee.

1
2
3
4
5
6
7
3. Inventory is a business word that describes the total amount of goods and/or material a company has on hand. Taking inventory means counting those goods and material. Taking inventory is an essential business practice. Factory owners need to know how many finished products are available for sale and if they have the parts and material to build those products. Car dealers often have high inventory. To move their old inventory, they often have sales, particularly at the end of the year when new car models are arriving.

1
2
3
4
5
6
7
8
4. The hierarchy of Latin honors describes three levels of student achievement. First is cum laude, which means "with honor." Next is magna cum laude. It means "with great honor." The highest honor is summa cum laude. It means "with the highest praise." A "summa" is a student who has demonstrated academic excellence and is at the top of his or her class. Barack Obama graduated magna cum laude from Harvard Law School. Natalie Portman graduated magna cum laude from the University of Pennsylvania while the rapper Ludacris graduated summa cum laude in business from Georgia State University.

1
2
3
4
5
5. Tea is the most widely consumed beverage in the world with coffee gaining in popularity. Of the two, tea offers the greatest health benefits. A cup of black tea is filled with anti-oxidants and cancer-fighting compounds, whereas a Harvard study revealed that coffee has no health benefits. Of the two, coffee is higher in caffeine while neither offers any nutritional value.

Exercise #3: Rhetorical Strategies → Level 3

Task: Identify five rhetorical strategies in each paragraph. Check your answers on page 170.

1. The animal kingdom is comprised of cold and warm-blooded animals. The body temperature of cold-blooded or ectothermic animals is regulated by the external environment while internal mechanisms keep the body temperature of warm-blooded or endothermic animals constant. Reptiles, such as lizards and snakes, are cold-blooded, whereas mammals, such as whales and humans, are warm-blooded. Most animals are warm-blooded; however, there are exceptions, such as bats and moles. Their body temperatures vary depending on whether or not they are active. Because warm-blooded animals generate body heat internally, they must eat 10 times more than cold-blooded animals. As a result, warm-blooded animals must be capable of finding food to meet this need. On the other hand, because cold-blood animals are heated by the sun's energy, they require less food.

2. Cloning is the process of making an exact copy of an original organism through asexual reproduction using one parent, whereas reproduction consists of two parents, a male and a female. The most famous cloned animal was Dolly the sheep; however, Dolly was not an exact replica of her parent. Genetic material from the donor cell into which Dolly's parents' DNA had to be inserted was .01 %. To clone Dolly, it took 277 donor eggs and 29 embryos before birth was achieved. Humans can be cloned; however, that idea remains controversial. Many believe it is unethical to harvest human donor eggs and experiment with embryos. Cloning extinct animals, such as the wooly mammoth, however, has gained popularity in recent years. Yet this too has raised serious issues, for bringing back extinct animals could drastically alter the natural order, especially if the animal cloned were a T-Rex.

3. Her name was Norma Jeane Baker. The world knew her as the movie star Marilyn Monroe. She was born in Los Angeles on June 1, 1926. As a child, Monroe spent most of her life in foster homes and an orphanage. At sixteen, she married for the first time but divorced soon after. It was then that she changed her name to Marilyn Monroe. During World War II, she worked in a factory where she met a photographer who took photos of her. Hollywood noticed and she soon had small movie roles that led to larger roles in comedies and dramas. By 1953, Monroe, famous for playing "dumb blondes," was starring in such movies as *Niagara*, *Gentlemen Prefer Blondes*, and Billy Wilder's *Some Like it Hot*. Monroe, the most popular sex symbol of the 1950's, married the baseball player Joe DiMaggio, then the playwright Arthur Miller. Both marriages ended in divorce. Marilyn Monroe died on August 5, 1962 at the age of 36 having battled depression, addiction, and anxiety all her life. Her last film was *The Misfits* (1961).

<u>Exercise #4</u>: Writing and Rhetorical Strategies

<u>Task</u>: Write about each topic using as many rhetorical strategies as you can.

1. TOEFL

   _____

2. friends

   _____

3. food

   _____

4. travel

   _____

5. money

   _____

6. technology

   _____

7. holidays

   _____

8. sports

   _____

9. home

   _____

10. love

   _____

 **Audio Track #1**

Exercise #5: Listening for Rhetorical Strategies

<u>Task</u>: Identify the rhetorical strategies in each sample. Check your answers and the tapescript on page 172.

1. _____

2. _____

3. _____

4. _____

5. _____

6. _____

7. _____

8. _____

9. _____

10. _____

11. _____

12. _____

13. _____

14. _____

15. _____

Reasons

Reasons are an important part of argument development and analysis, and TOEFL too. You can create a reason by using the rhetorical strategy of cause-and-effect to answer the question why, for example:

1. Question: Why did Daisy get a high TOEFL score?

   or...   What was the reason (the cause and the effect) she got a high score?

   Answer: Because Daisy studied hard (cause), she got a high score (effect).
   That is the reason (cause = studied hard + effect = high score).

....

2. Question: Why is the ice melting at the South Pole?

   Answer: Because of global warming (cause), the ice is melting (effect).
   That is the reason (cause = global warming + effect = ice is melting).

....

3. Betty: Why do you want to go for pizza? I thought you wanted sushi.

   Robert: Because the last time I ate sushi (cause), I was sick (effect).

   Betty: That's a good reason (to want pizza instead of sushi).

   Robert: Also, pizza (buying and eating pizza = cause) is cheaper (effect).

   Betty: Okay. I'm persuaded (your cause-and-effect reasoning has con-evinced me). Let's go. I'm starving.

....

1
2
3
4
5
6

4. Teacher: Good morning, class. Today we are going to talk about rats and why they are so successful living in urban environments. One reason they are so successful (effect) is that they can eat anything (cause). Another reason why rats thrive in urban environments (effect) is because they breed often (cause). Those are a few of the reasons (causes and effects) we will talk about this morning.

Exercise #6: Reasons → Level 1

Task: Identify the cause-and-effect reason in the following. Remember: A reason answers the question why. Check your answers on page 175.

1. Joey failed the test because he never went to class.

2. The plant didn't get enough sun and water, so it died.

_____

3. Use examples to make an argument more persuasive.

_____

4. Susan cried when her pet dog Leo died.

_____

5. The band had to cancel the show because they didn't sell enough tickets.

_____

6. Steve was late for work because he forgot to set his alarm clock.

_____

7. The students' grades improved because the teacher gave them extra homework.

_____

8. The company is moving to a smaller city to save money.

_____

9. Lily decided to buy a new computer when her old computer crashed.

_____

10. Blame our poor sales on the economy slowing down.

_____

11. The drought in California is due to a lack of rain.

_____

12. Cigarettes cause cancer and myriad other life-threatening diseases.

_____

13. Tom's argument failed to persuade his parents.

_____

14. The heavy rain flooded many rivers.

_____

15. Many people get married because they want to raise a family.

_____

Exercise #7: Reasons → Level 2

Task: Identify the cause-and-effect reasoning in each. Remember: A reason answers the question why. Check your answers on page 176.

1. If provoked, a wild animal, such as a bear or a wolf, will attack.

_____

2. Without a life-support system, man can't survive in space.

_____

3. Adding fertilizer to crops will substantially increase the per-acre yield.

_____

4. Long ago, a comet streaking across the night sky caused great consternation among the populace, as comets were harbingers of misfortune.

_____

5. Stress is robbing Stan of sleep and the ability to focus at work.

_____

6. An asteroid struck Earth millions of years ago and wiped out the dinosaurs.

_____

7. Properly inflated tires will ensure better gas mileage and safety.

_____

8. To avoid contracting malaria, take malaria pills when visiting high-risk zones.

_____

9. Consumers will protest if the government imposes a tariff on imported products, like smartphones and computers.

_____

10. Practice charity, for it is a gift that will change your life.

_____

11. The aroma of the voodoo lily smells like rotting flesh to attract pollinating flies.

_____

12. The company should hire more accountants to improve its record keeping.

_____

13. The sky is blue because molecules in the air scatter blue light more than red.

_____

14. The Shrike is nicknamed "the butcher bird" because after it catches a meal, such as a mouse, it impales it on a branch or thorn for easier consumption.

_____

15. Bullying is a growing social problem that can have life-long effects on a child's self-esteem.

_____

Exercise #8: Reasons → Level 3

Task: Identify examples of cause-and-effect reasoning in each passage. Remember: A reason answers the question why. Check your answers on page 176.

1 1. An avalanche, also called a snow slide or snow slip, is a great accumulation of
2   snow and ice that travels rapidly down a mountainside. Most avalanches occur
3   without warning. Why do they start? First, there is so much snow that gravity
4   pulls it down thus causing a chain reaction in which the weight of the falling
5   snow starts to push other snow downhill. The second cause is metamorphic.

6	Rocks are heated by the sun causing ice and snow to melt. The melting causes
7	great sheets of snow to move resulting in an avalanche. Other causes are rain,
8	earthquakes, and rock fall. To form, an avalanche needs a slope with an angle
9	shallow enough to hold snow yet steep enough to accelerate the snow once it
10	starts moving. Ninety-percent of avalanches are caused by skiers or snow-
11	boarders in an avalanche zone. They break up the snowpack which starts the
12	snow moving downhill. Once the avalanche stops, the snow sets like concrete.
13	Bodily movement is next to impossible. If dug out within fifteen minutes, you
14	will survive. After two hours, very few survive. If caught in an avalanche, try
15	and get off the slab, the snowpack that is moving. Skiers and snowboards
16	should go straight downhill to try and outrace the snow. If you can't escape,
17	hold on to a tree if possible. Or swim hard. The human body is heavy and will
18	sink. Once the slide stops, create a breathing space, then punch a hand up to
19	signal your location.

1	2. On June 18, 1815, the Napoleonic Era in Europe ended with Napoleon Bona-
2	parte's defeat at the Battle of Waterloo. Historians argue that Napoleon, one of
3	the greatest military minds in history, was defeated for myriad reasons. First,
4	Napoleon, with 73,000 troops, waited too long to attack the Duke of Wellington
5	with 68,000 men. Napoleon, history records, wanted to let the rain-soaked
6	ground dry out first, but in delaying, he gave time for Prussian General Blucher
7	to bring forward his 50,000 strong army. By noon, the time Napoleon ordered
8	the attack, he was facing a combined British-Prussian army of over 118,000.
9	Next, Napoleon took the offensive. He rolled wave after wave of his elite French
10	forces against Wellington's stalwart defenses and eventually paid the price. An-
11	other reason why Napoleon was defeated at Waterloo is more prosaic: hemor-
12	rhoids. Hemorrhoids are an inflation of blood vessels that prevent the afflicted
13	from sitting down. Historians argue that a painful bout of hemorrhoids prevent-
14	ed Napoleon from riding his horse that day. As a result, he could not survey the
15	battlefield thus he was fighting blind. Whether this is true or not we may never
16	know. Yet this is known. After the battle, 41,000 dead remained on the field.
17	Soon they were beset by locals hunting for teeth, which they extracted and sold
18	to dentists, for false teeth were in high demand. These false teeth became
19	known as Waterloo teeth, and were still being sold in 1860, forty-five years after
20	Waterloo, a battle that changed history.

Exercise #9: Writing and Reasons

Task: Use the following topics to write a sentence using a reason based on cause-and-effect.

1. divorce

_____

2. success

_____

3. happiness

_____

4. mystery

_____

5. facebook

_____

6. boss

_____

7. police

_____

8. Paris

_____

9. parents

_____

10. sugar

_____

 **Audio Track #2**

Exercise #10: Listening for Reasons

Task: Identify examples of cause-and-effect reasoning in each passage. Remember: A reason answers the questions why. The answers and tapescript are on page 177.

1. _____

2. _____

3. _____

4. _____

5. _____

6. _____

7. _____

8. _____

9. _____

10. _____

11. _____

12. _____

13. _____

14. _____

15. _____

16. _____

17. _____

18. _____

19. _____

20. _____

Inferring → Reading Between the Lines

Often when reading or listening to an argument, the facts are clearly stated. Because the facts are clearly stated, you can make direct conclusions, for example:

Fact: *Mary didn't eat breakfast.* Direct conclusion = *Mary is hungry.*

However, sometimes you must make conclusions by reading between the lines. This process is called inferring. To infer means to make a conclusion based on the facts provided. Look at the following example.

Fact: *Joe doesn't eat red meat.* Inferred Conclusion = ?

What can we infer (conclude) about Joe? We can infer that: 1) Joe is on a diet, or; 2) he is a vegetarian, or; 3) he only eats white meat, such as chicken, pork, and/or fish. Note how we are making conclusions about Joe by inferring. In other words, we are reading between the lines. Look at the next example.

Fact: *The car Roberto wanted to buy was more expensive than he thought.*

What can we infer from this statement? We can infer that: 1) Roberto was not expecting a higher price for the car, or; 2) he was surprised/disappointed when he learned the real price of the car, or; 3) he did not buy the car because he could not afford it, or; 4) he did not buy the car because he thought it was too expensive, or; 5) he might get a loan to pay for it.

- **REMEMBER:** *Being able to infer is an essential TOEFL skill.*

Exercise #11: Inferring → Level 1

Task: What can you infer from the following? Check your answers on page 178.

1. The shoes Allen buys online never fit.

_____

2. Eva is always late for work.

_____

3. Anna got a perfect TOEFL score.

_____

4. Beth doesn't use anti-virus software.

_____

5. Joey has been married five times.

_____

6. Jim sneezes whenever a cat is near.

_____

7. Erika claims she has seen many ghosts.

_____

8. Bridget got another speeding ticket.

_____

9. Harvard and Yale accept only the top students in the world.

_____

10. Betty never answers Bobby's emails.

_____

11. Ali fell asleep in class.

_____

12. Jana got a raise at work.

_____

13. Allen never tells the truth.

_____

14. Katy can't swim.

_____

15. George told his students they could go home early.

_____

Exercise #12: Inferring → Level 2

Task: What can you infer from the following? Check your answers on page 181.

1. Many aquariums have tried to keep a great white shark but each attempt has ended in failure, the great white dying soon after it was displayed.

2. Otzi the Iceman, the 5,000-year-old body found alone and frozen in ice in the Austrian Alps, had an arrow in his back.

3. Mount Everest is the highest mountain on Earth. To date, more than 250 people have died trying to climb it.

4. When Microsoft introduced its new Windows operating software in 1995, many thought it looked exactly like Apple's operating system.

5. Donald Trump accused President Barack Obama of not being born in America thus was not eligible to be president; however, Trump never produced any evidence to support his claim even after five years.

6. On July 2, 1937, Emily Earhart was attempting to be the first women to fly around the world when her plane disappeared over the Pacific Ocean. Years later, in 2012, the heel of her shoe was found on remote Nikumaroro Island.

7. Hachiko was a dog who waited for his master every day in front Shibuya Station in Tokyo. When his master died in 1925, Hachiko continued to wait. Hachiko died still waiting in 1935.

8. When the stock market crashed in 1929, many on Wall Street jumped out of windows to their deaths.

---

9. To this day, some Americans say that the American Civil War was fought to free the slaves while others say it was fought to defend states' rights.

---

10. In America, the thumbs-up sign means "Okay" or "good" while in other countries, this same sign has a negative meaning.

---

11. Warren Buffet, the richest man in America, eats junk food every day. He has a particular fondness for Cheetos and Coke.

---

12. When Annie and Lily went for a walk in the forest, they saw a deer with two fawns.

---

13. Scientists refuse to investigate, or even consider, evidence of UFOs.

---

14. It takes one gallon of water to grow one almond and five gallons for one walnut.

---

15. The average internet user spends less than 20 seconds on a web site before clicking over to another site. The result is the mind has little or no time to concentrate. This, doctors say, reduces the brain's ability to retain information in the long-term memory.

Exercise #13: Inferring → Level 3

Task: What can you infer from the following? Check your answers on page 184.

1. William Shakespeare is considered the greatest writer in the English language. He was born in Stratford in April 1563, the exact date not known. In 1582, when he was eighteen, he married Anne Hathaway. They had three children. Around 1588, Shakespeare moved his family to London where he went on to write 38 plays, including *Hamlet, Romeo and Juliet*, and *Othello*. Yet in 1598, the Stratford town record describes resident William Shakespeare as a grain hoarder and a tax dodger. When he died in 1616, his death went unnoticed while lesser writers were given elaborate funerals attended by royalty. Moreover, the poetry on his headstone is of inferior quality. In his will, he made no mention of his plays or poems or manuscripts, or how to dispose of them. Indeed, there is no evidence that Shakespeare ever wrote a letter or that he was even literate. Six signatures are the only lasting evidence; three are incomplete while the other three are barely legible. His wife was illiterate as were those around him. All this stands in stark contrast to the London playwright whose plays reference a world of knowledge, including Greek philosophy and tragedy, and moreover, political intrigue. He knew naval and military strategy and had an intimate knowledge of royal pastimes, including the art of falconry. The original Shakespeare monument in Stratford did not show a writer holding a quill or a book. Instead, it showed a man holding a bag grain, indicating that he was a grain merchant. Some argue that the real William Shakespeare was Edward de Vere, Earl of Oxford, and that for political and social reasons, he had to conceal his identity. De Vere was a noted patron of the arts, poet and playwright. His erratic and volatile behavior (he impregnated one of Elizabeth 1's maids of honor) got him exiled from court, yet he returned to favor and went on to become Elizabeth's "the most excellent of Elizabeth's courtier poets."

2. Light travels at 186,282 miles per second or 299,792 kilometers. A light-year is the distance light travels in one year. That distance is 6 trillion miles or 9 trillion kilometers. The observable universe, that which is known to mankind, is a staggering 92 billion light-years in diameter. Within that space are billions of galaxies, stars, and planets. Our galaxy, the Milk Way, is 100,000 light-years in diameter. It contains approximately 400 billion star systems like our sun and its planets. How many galaxies are there? One scientist said, "There are more galaxies in the universe than there are grains of sand on all the beaches of Earth." As you can see, the universe is huge, so much so that it is hard to imagine just how big. And that is only the known universe. But all this raises an interesting question: Are we humans on planet Earth the only life form in the universe?

Exercise #14: Writing and Inferring

<u>Task</u>: Write sentences in which your reader must infer your meaning. The first one has been done for you. The topic is ice cream. See page 186 for sample answers.

1. <u>ice cream</u> = *Fred ate all the ice cream - again!*
    <u>What can we infer</u>? *Fred loves ice cream; Fred has a sweet tooth; Fred is selfish.*

2. money _____

3. reef _____

4. married _____

5. dictionary _____

6. solution _____

7. sick _____

8. bank _____

9. airplane _____

10. bake _____

11. lion _____

12. diet _____

13. work _____

14. accident _____

15. music _____

 **Audio Track #3**

Exercise #15: Listening and Inferring

<u>Task</u>: What is each sample inferring? Your inferences will vary. See page 189 for the answers and tape script.

1. _____

2. _____

3. _____

4. _____

5. _____

6. _____

7. _____

8. _____

9. _____

10. _____

11. _____

12. _____

13. _____

14. _____

15. _____

Topic + Controlling Idea

Every sentence, paragraph, and argument has a topic and a controlling idea. The topic is the main subject. The controlling idea is what the topic is about. Look at the following sentence.

Americans love hamburgers.

In this sentence, the topic is *Americans*. To find the controlling idea, ask, "What about Americans?" <u>Answer</u>: *love hamburgers*. Look at the next example.

Barack Obama was the first black president of the United States.

The topic is *Barack Obama*. What about him? Controlling idea = *was the first black president of the United States.*

- **REMEMBER:** *Being able to identify the topic and the controlling idea is an essential TOEFL and IELTS skill.*

Exercise #16: Topic + Controlling Idea → Level 1

<u>Task</u>: Identify the topic and controlling idea in each. Check your answers on page page 193.

1. David and Susan bought a new house.

_____

2. Traveling is so much fun.

_____

3. Annie believes that hard work leads to success.

_____

4. Robins are the first birds to return in spring.

_____

5. The oldest city in the United States is St. Augustine in Florida.

_____

6. Contrary to popular belief, cats and dogs are not natural enemies.

_____

7. Skiing and snowboarding are two popular winter sports.

_____

8. After Professor Smith read Brenda's essay, he told her it was excellent.

_____

9. The first great battle of the American Civil War was the battle of Bull Run.

_____

10. A good example of a hard worker is Paul.

_____

11. Professional athletes are paid too much.

_____

12. Being accepted into Harvard was not what Lucy expected.

_____

13. In America, pizza is round, whereas in many countries, it is square.

_____

14. Studying for TOEFL takes time and preparation.

_____

15. The process of buying a house can be stressful.

_____

16. Making a wish is said to bring good luck.

_____

Exercise #17: Topic + Controlling Idea → Level 2

Task: Identify the topic and controlling idea in each. Check your answers on page page 194.

1. The assassination of archduke Franz Ferdinand in Sarajevo on June 28, 1914 was the spark that ignited the First World War.

2. Inasmuch as is a synonym for because.

3. Yellow fever is a blood disease transmitted by mosquitoes to humans.

4. If Mary had known that Charles was going to be at the party, she would not have gone.

5. Defined, a polar vortex is a mass of Arctic air that moves south in winter and settles over Canada and the United States, bringing high winds and dangerously low temperatures.

6. Albert Einstein said, "The true sign of intelligence is not knowledge but imagination."

7. The Elbe River in Spain is home to world-record catfish.

8. George believes that life exists in the universe and that one day we will find it while Federica believes that life does not exist, that humans are the only life form in the universe.

9. The air pollution is so bad in Beijing, the airport often shuts down inasmuch as planes cannot take off or land due to reduced visibility.

---

10. Chemistry and biology were the subjects Clarissa enjoyed the most in high school, whereas English and French were the subjects she liked the least.

---

11. Cancer, emphysema, and chronic bronchitis are just a few of the crippling diseases you can get from smoking.

---

12. The professors discussed the issue brought before them by the students and decided that the dean should hear about it and decide for herself what to do.

---

13. Most countries have one national sport however Canada has two. Hockey is Canada's national winter sport while lacrosse is the national summer sport.

---

14. Homo Sapiens is the scientific name for humans.

---

15. Sleeplessness, decreased urine output, headaches, and constipation are all signs of dehydration. How can you remedy dehydration? Drink more water.

Exercise #18: Topic + Controlling Idea → Level 3

Task: Identify the topic and the controlling idea in each. Check your answers on page 196.

1. U.K. lawyers are called barristers and solicitors, whereas in America, a lawyer is both a barrister and a solicitor.

---

2. Is the Chicxulub Crater under the Yucatan Peninsula in Mexico evidence of the asteroid that struck the Earth and wiped out the dinosaurs? That theory, while indeed compelling, remains controversial.

---

3. A major event in the world of science was Nicolaus Copernicus' formulating of a model of the universe that placed the sun, not the Earth, at the center of our solar system.

---

4. In order to reach their breeding grounds, wildebeest, or gnus, must overcome many obstacles, including the Mara River where crocodiles lie in wait.

---

5. A complex neuro-physiological process is left-right discrimination. For most, it is second nature; however, many struggle telling their left from their right. Why is that?

---

6. Leonardo da Vinci is an acknowledged genius, a true Renaissance man who designed myriad revolutionary ideas, such as the first helicopter; however, as a painter, historical records confirm that he disappointed many of his patrons by failing to finish a work on time or not at all. That such few da Vinci paintings exist underscores this fact.

---

7. Socrates (470-399 BC) was a Greek philosopher famous for developing what today is known as the Socratic method, a system of cooperative argumentative dialogue between individuals aimed at stimulating critical thinking through the asking and answering of questions. This dialectal method of discourse between opposing viewpoints remains the cornerstone of the western educational tradition.

---

8. In 1941, a German military officer in Russia filmed a woolly mammoth, an animal that had supposedly been extinct for over 10,000 years. However, it was later proven that the film was indeed a hoax.

---

9. They are found on every continent but Antarctica and instill fear in many. They can spin silken webs five times stronger than steel. They have eight legs and blue blood. They can grow as wide as eleven inches and as small as the head of a pin. Some are so deadly one bite will kill you while others make excellent pets. Some are considered living fossils while others can run two feet per second. Some give presents while some can jump forty times their body length. Contrary to popular belief, they are not insects, like flies and ants. Instead, they are arachnids or spiders.

---

10. Past is prologue.

---

11. There are many firsts in history: the first car, the first radio, the first vaccine. However, few firsts compare to the introduction of the printing press in 1468 by Johannes Gutenberg, a German blacksmith. Gutenberg created mechanical movable type printing. The result was the Bible could be mass produced. This allowed more people to read and ultimately created the modern, knowledge-based world we know today.

---

12. Look up? What do you see? Straight white lines crisscrossing the clear blue sky. Are they clouds? Yes. More specifically, they are jet contrails. Let me explain. Jets fly at extremely high altitudes where it is very cold, as cold as -50 C. The hot exhaust of the jet's engines contains a lot of water. When that water hits the cold ambient air, it condenses and freezes creating ice crystals. Those crystals are jet contrails.

---

13. The Harrier, or "jump jet", is a British combat jet capable of vertical takeoff and landing. It gets its name from the species of diurnal hawks called harriers, which form the Circinae sub-family of the Accipitridae family of birds of prey.

---

14. Visit the cooking oil section in your local grocery store and you will find myriad oils with which to cook and season. Of those oils, olive oil is the healthiest. It is high in the phytonutrient oleocanthal, which mimics the anti-inflammatory effects of ibuprofen. This can aid in cancer prevention and reduce joint pain. Olive oil can also reduce the levels of blood cholesterol, LDL-cholesterol, and triglycerides while not altering the level of HDL-cholesterol.

---

15. Modern political theory owes much to *The Prince*, a book by Niccolo Machiavelli in which Machiavelli describes the ideal leader, a person lacking in morals in order to do whatever it takes to succeed, a man such as Donald Trump.

Exercise #19: Writing → Topic + Controlling Idea

Task: Write a *controlling idea* for each topic. The first one has been done for you.

1. Hollywood *is where movies are made*.

2. The North Pole

3. Oxford University

4. museums

5. The Sahara Desert

6. Steve Jobs and Bill Gates

7. coffee

8. Instagram

9. dieting

10. rock and roll

_____

11. global warming

_____

12. Friday

_____

13. finding a job

_____

14. malware

_____

15. parents

_____

Audio Track #4

Exercise #20: Listening → Topic + Controlling Idea

Task: Identify the topic and the controlling idea in each. Check your answers and the tapescript on page 199.

1. _____

2. _____

3. _____

4. _____

5. _____

6. _____

7. _____

8. _____

9. _____

10. _____

11. _____

12. _____

13. _____

14. _____

15. _____

Notes

_____
_____
_____
_____
_____
_____
_____
_____
_____
_____

Writing a Personal Essay

Now that you have the tools to write an essay, let's start writing. We begin with the personal essay. The personal essay is the first essay (argument) American students learn how to write. American students start writing personal essays in middle school and continue to write them in high school and in college. A master's thesis and a PhD dissertation are, despite their fancy names, just long personal essays. For each, you develop an original argument (personal idea) and support it with a lot of illustrations and reasons based on research. TOEFL knows this. That is why the last task on the TOEFL test is the independent writing task or personal essay. By giving you this task, TOEFL wants to know if you know how to write the most popular essay type in the American educational system: the personal essay.

To write a basic proficient personal essay, follow these steps.

Subjective Thesis → Persuading an Audience

A personal essay starts with your opinion. Your opinion is what you believe. Your opinion is also called a *subjective thesis*. Subjective means you are using first person grammar (*I, me, mine...*) to write your thesis, for example: *I believe that we need zoos.* Some people, however, do not believe that we need zoos. That is their opinion, their claim, their subjective thesis.

- **REMEMBER:** *The purpose of a personal essay is to persuade your audience that what you believe is right, true, possible, or all three.*

A subjective thesis often starts with a **_signal phrase_**, for example:

Personally, I believe that we need more zoos.

Below are common signal phrases that introduce a subjective thesis.

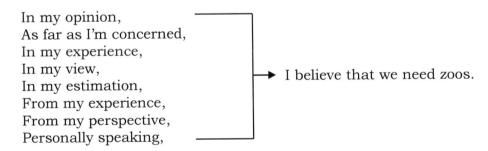

In my opinion,
As far as I'm concerned,
In my experience,
In my view,
In my estimation,
From my experience,
From my perspective,
Personally speaking,

I believe that we need zoos.

<u>Identifying a Subjective Thesis</u> → **Rules Checklist**

As you know, a subjective thesis starts a personal essay. Yet how do you know if what you are writing or saying is indeed a subjective thesis? Use the rules checklist below. Apply these rules to the following statement to determine if it is a subjective thesis or not.

<u>Statement</u>: *Personally, I believe that we need zoos.*

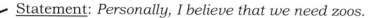

1) A subjective thesis is arguable. Is this statement arguable?
   ✓ Yes. Some believe that wild animals should be free not caged.

2) A subjective thesis has one topic only. Does this statement have one topic?
   ✓ Yes: topic = "zoos".

3) A subjective thesis has a topic and a controlling idea. Does this statement have a topic and a controlling idea?
   ✓ Yes: topic = "zoos"; controlling idea = "we need".

4) A subjective thesis is supportable. Is this statement supportable? Can it be developed with body paragraph examples?
   ✓ Yes. See page 54.

5) A subjective thesis is a grammatically complete sentence. Is this statement a grammatically complete sentence?
   ✓ Yes. It has a subject (I...) and a predicate (...believe that we need zoos). A sentence fragment is not a thesis, for example: *Steve Jobs: genius.*

6) A subjective thesis is not a question. Is this statement a question?
   ✓ No. A subjective thesis is never a question. A *rhetorical question*, however, often introduces the topic the subjective thesis will argue, for example: *"<u>Do we need zoos</u>? Yes. Personally, I believe that we need zoos."*

7) A subjective thesis is not a fact. Is this statement a fact?
   ✓ No. This statement is arguable. A fact, in contrast, is not arguable, for example: *"A zoo is place where people can safely view protected wild animals."* This statement is a fact thus not arguable.

8) A subjective thesis is not an announcement. Is this statement an announcement?
   ✓ No. *"Today, I am going to talk about zoos"* is an announcement. An announcement is a fact thus not arguable.

9) A subjective thesis is stated academically, and the controlling idea is developable. Is this statement stated academically? Is the controlling idea developable?
   ✓ Yes. Simply stating a like or a dislike is not a thesis, for example: *"Zoos are great!"* This is indeed an opinion; however, it is not stated academically. Moreover, the controlling idea is not specific enough.

So what is the conclusion? Is *Personally, I believe that we need zoos* a subjective thesis? Yes. Why? Because it follows the rules in the subjective thesis checklist on the previous page.

- **REMEMBER:** *A thesis is also called a claim or a position.*

Subjective Thesis → No Signal Phrase

A subjective thesis will not always start with a *signal phrase* followed by *a personal pronoun* and *a stative verb*, for example:

> *Personally, I believe that...*

However, if the statement is arguable—and it follows the subjective thesis rules checklist—then we can infer that it is the writer's/speaker's claim, for example:

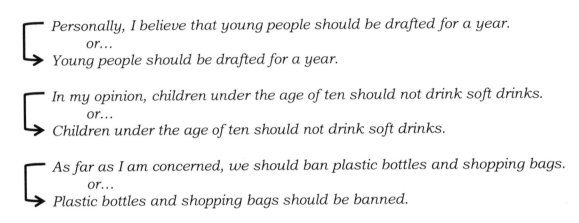

Personally, I believe that young people should be drafted for a year.
or...
Young people should be drafted for a year.

In my opinion, children under the age of ten should not drink soft drinks.
or...
Children under the age of ten should not drink soft drinks.

As far as I am concerned, we should ban plastic bottles and shopping bags.
or...
Plastic bottles and shopping bags should be banned.

Subjective Thesis → Well-Developed

A well-developed, subjective thesis will score higher, for example:

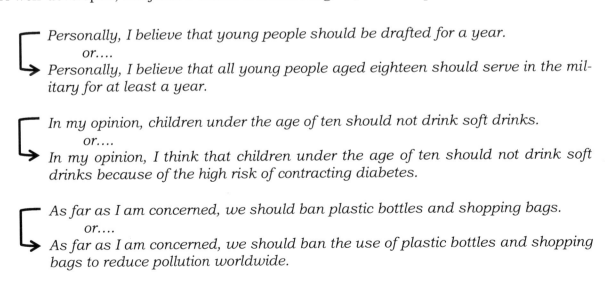

Personally, I believe that young people should be drafted for a year.
or....
Personally, I believe that all young people aged eighteen should serve in the military for at least a year.

In my opinion, children under the age of ten should not drink soft drinks.
or....
In my opinion, I think that children under the age of ten should not drink soft drinks because of the high risk of contracting diabetes.

As far as I am concerned, we should ban plastic bottles and shopping bags.
or....
As far as I am concerned, we should ban the use of plastic bottles and shopping bags to reduce pollution worldwide.

<u>Subjective Writing</u> → Short Personal Essay

The purpose of a personal essay is to persuade an audience. At school, your audience is your fellow students and teachers. For TOEFL, you also have an audience: two official ETS writing raters. However, on test day, your job is not to persuade the two raters with your personal essay. Why not? For good reason. If the raters do not like your opinion—if they think <u>we don't need zoos</u>, but you think we do—the raters could give you a zero simply because they disagree. That would not be fair. It is not fair because it is a subjective evaluation, and subjective rater evaluations are biased. ETS knows this and trains its raters to rate objectively without bias or opinion. That means the raters do not care about the topic or your opinion. They are neutral. Their job is to evaluate how well you can organize your ideas when writing.

A basic personal essay has a three-part structure, as illustrated below. Each part serves a specific function in the argument development process.

1. introduction ⟶ introduces your subjective thesis
2. body ⟶ examples to support your thesis
3. conclusion ⟶ restates your thesis

Next, let's write a short personal essay. First, we need a prompt. A prompt tells you what to write about, for example:

Prompt: *We need zoos. What is your position? Use an example and a reason to develop your argument.*

Before you write, make sure you understand the prompt. Do so by analyzing each part of the prompt. Note below how each part of the prompt has a purpose.

Prompt: *We need zoos.*

> Analysis: The topic is "zoos." The controlling ideas is "We need..." Need means "have a purpose" or "have value."

Prompt: *What is your position?*

> Analysis: What is your position means what is your opinion. Do you think we need zoos or not? Answer this question by stating your opinion in writing using a subjective thesis.

Prompt: *Use an example...*

> Analysis: This means use the rhetorical strategy of illustration to develop and support your subjective thesis with a personal experience example.

Prompt: *...and a reason to develop your argument.*

> Analysis: This means use the rhetorical strategy of cause-and-effect to create a reason to support your subjective thesis.

After you analyze the prompt, and understand what you must write about, it is time to write. First, state your subjective thesis in the introduction, for example:

introduction ➔ Personally, I believe that we need zoos.

Do not worry about developing your introduction with a hook. A hook capture's your reader's attention. However, a hook is not the starting point of your argument. Your subjective thesis is the starting point. Remember: *No thesis, no argument.*

Next, add a rhetorical **Why.**

introduction ➔ Personally, I believe that we need zoos. **Why?**

Next, answer Why.

introduction ➔ Personally, I believe that we need zoos. Why? We need them because they are educational.

Often the answer to why is shortened to a *sentence fragment*, for example:

introduction ➔ Personally, I believe that we need zoos. Why? *Because they are educational.*

A fragment is not a complete sentence. Because fragments are not complete sentences, you have been taught not to use them. However, when answering a rhetorical-why question, you can use a sentence fragment. This type of fragment is called a rhetorical fragment. Rhetorical fragments are used for emphasis when arguing.

Note how the rhetorical fragment contains a **cause**-and-*effect* reason.

introduction ➔ Personally, I believe that we need zoos. Why? Because **they** (having zoos = cause) *are educational* (effect).

Next, develop a body paragraph. In the body paragraph, develop a personal example to support your thesis and reason. Use narration, description, compare-and-contrast, and other rhetorical strategies when developing, for example (note: para means paragraph):

body para ➔ For example, when I was twelve, my teacher took us to the zoo in Toronto. I had never seen wild animals before. I had just read about them in books and seen them on the TV. But seeing them in real life was amazing, especially the lions. On TV, they looked so small, but when I saw them live, they were really big. By going to the zoo, you can definitely learn something new.

Next, add a conclusion. Start with a <u>signal phrase</u>, then restate your thesis.

conclusion ➜ <u>In conclusion</u>, I believe that we need zoos because they are educational.

Finished! You now have a short personal essay with a clear three-part structure. That is what the writing raters are trained to look for.

introduction ➜ Personally, I believe that we need zoos. Why? Because they are educational.

body para ➜ For example, when I was twelve, my teacher took us to the zoo in Toronto. I had never seen wild animals before. I had just read about them in books and seen them on the TV. But seeing them in real life was amazing, especially the lions. On TV, they looked so small, but when I saw them live, they were really big. By going to the zoo, you can definitely learn something new.

conclusion ➜ In conclusion, I believe that we need zoos because they are educational.

Next, let's analyze this short personal essay for proficiency. First, does this essay answer the prompt? Let's check and see using the prompt.

Prompt ➜ *We need zoos. What is your position?*

introduction ➜ Personally, I believe that we need zoos. Why? Because they are educational.

✓ <u>Analysis</u>: The writer's thesis is clear and arguable. Also, it is a subjective thesis according to the thesis rules checklist on page 47.

Prompt ➜ *Use an example...*

body para ➜ For example, when I was twelve, my teacher took us to the zoo in Toronto. I had never seen wild animals before. I had just read about them in books and seen them on the TV. But seeing them in real life was amazing, especially the lions. On TV, they looked so small, but when I saw them live, they were really big. By going to the zoo, you can definitely learn something new.

✓ <u>Analysis</u>: The example is well-developed and supports the thesis.

Prompt ➜ *...and a <u>reason</u> to develop your argument.*

body para ➜ For example, when I was twelve, my teacher took us to the zoo in Toronto. I had never seen wild animals before. I had just read about them in books and seen them on the TV. But seeing them in real life was amazing, especially the lions. On TV, they looked so small, but when I saw them live, they were really big.

By going to the zoo, *you can definitely learn something new.*

✓ Analysis: The sentence above is a **cause**-and-*effect* reason that topically supports the thesis.

conclusion ➜ In conclusion, I believe that we need zoos because they are educational.

✓ Analysis: The conclusion topically connects with the thesis in the introduction, with the body paragraph example, and with the reason in the conclusion.

As you can see, this short personal essay is doing everything right. In other words, it is proficient. Proficient means the writer has demonstrated skill and knowledge when writing a short personal essay. That is what the writing raters are trained to look for.

Exercise #21: Rhetorical Strategy Analysis

Task: In the short personal essay below, identify the rhetorical strategies used to develop the argument. Check your answers on page 201.

1	introduction ➜	Personally, I think that we need zoos. Why? Because they are
2		educational.
3		
4	body para ➜	For example, when I was twelve, my teacher took us to the zoo
5		in Toronto. I had never seen wild animals before. I had just
6		read about them in books and seen them on the TV. But seeing
7		them in real life was amazing, especially the lions. On TV, they
8		looked so small, but when I saw them live, they were really big.
9		By going to the zoo, you can definitely learn something new.
10		
11	conclusion ➜	In conclusion, I believe that we need zoos because they are edu-
12		cational.

Exercise #22: Writing Short Personal Essays

Task: Write a short, three-part personal essay like the one illustrated above in Exercise #21. Use the topics below, or topics of your own choosing. You have 15 minutes to complete each task.

1. Fast food is good for you. What is your position? Use an example and a reason to develop your argument.

2. Winter is the best season. What is your position? Use an example and a reason to develop your argument.

3. One word can change your life. What is your position? Use an example and a reason to develop your argument.

4. Which area of English should you improve? Use an example and a reason to develop your argument.

5. Is owning a smartphone necessary? Why? Use an example and a reason to develop your argument.

6. A dictionary is very useful. What is your position? Use an example and a reason to develop your argument.

7. What is a good way to relax? Why? Use an example and a reason to develop your argument.

8. A teacher can be a great influence. What is your position? Use an example and a reason to develop your argument.

9. Everyone needs more time. What is your position? Use an example and a reason to develop your argument.

10. Taking a test is stressful. What is your position? Use an example and a reason to develop your argument.

11. Texting is dangerous. What is your position? Use an example and a reason to develop your argument.

12. Everyone who is smart went to college. What is your position? Use an example and a reason to develop your argument.

13. Young people can teach the older generation new ideas. What is your position? Use an example and a reason to develop your argument.

14. TOEFL is easy. What is your position? Use an example and a reason to develop your argument.

15. You should see a dentist every six months. What is your position? Use an example and a reason to develop your argument.

16. Good grades are important. What is your position? Use an example and a reason to develop your argument.

17. The weather can affect your mood. What is your position? Use an example and a reason to develop your argument.

18. A friend can change your life. What is your position? Use an example and a reason to develop your argument.

19. Being late can cause problems. What is your position? Use an example and a reason to develop your argument.

20. Thrift is best. What is your position? Use an example and a reason to develop your argument.

TOEFL Independent Essay → The 5-Paragraph Essay

The short personal essay on page 52 (Exercise #21) is proficient. It demonstrates that you understand how to write a short personal essay. Great. However, for TOEFL, that essay—even though it is proficient—is too short. The raters want to see a longer essay. Longer means more reasons. More reasons means more examples and more topic development to support your thesis. You can add as many examples as you want. However, three body paragraphs is enough, as illustrated below. You now have a classic 5-paragraph, American-style personal essay. TOEFL calls it the independent essay or independent writing task.

1 2	<u>introduction</u> →	Personally, I believe that we need zoos. Why? For many reasons.
3 4 5 6 7 8 9	<u>body para #1</u> →	First, when I was twelve, my teacher took us to the zoo in Toronto. I had never seen wild animals before. I had just read about them in books and seen them on the TV. But seeing them in real life was amazing, especially the lions. On TV, they looked so small, but when I saw them live, they were really big. By going to the zoo, you can definitely learn something new.
10 11 12 13 14 15	<u>body para #2</u> →	Next, I now have a family and we always go to the zoo every summer. My wife makes picnic and we spend all day there. My kids love taking pictures and learning all about the animals, especially the gorillas. Being outside is good for my children. Best of all, they can leave the internet and the TV at home.
16 17 18 19 20 21 22	<u>body para #3</u> →	Finally, zoos look after endangered animals like pandas. I saw two in the Washington DC zoo last year and they had a baby. If there were no zoos, the pandas would disappear because we are taking their land away. However, in a zoo the pandas are safe. It is not perfect, but without zoos there might not be any pandas left.
23 24	<u>conclusion</u> →	In conclusion, I believe that we need zoos for many reasons.

- **REMEMBER:** *Many TOEFL students think their personal essays need a hook in the introduction. A hook is a rhetorical strategy. Its purpose is to grab (hook) the reader's attention. A hook also develops the introduction. However, in my experience as a TOEFL author and instructor, I find that TOEFL students spend far too much time worrying about writing hooks and not enough time writing proficient opinions. The result is they run out of time and do not finish writing their essays. Worse, the hook they wrote lacks proficiency, is too long, and is not topically connected to the thesis.*

- **REMEMBER:** *For pre-TOEFL students, I recommend that you focus on mastering the personal essay first and forget about hooks. If you want more information on advanced argument strategies, see my book <u>TOEFL Strategies A Complete Guide to the iBT</u> by NovaPress.net.*

Exercise #23: Writing TOEFL Independent Essays

<u>Task:</u> Write TOEFL independent essays like the one illustrated on the previous page. You have 30 minutes for each essay.

1. Before an important exam, do you think it is better to prepare for a long time or only for a few days? Give examples and reasons to support your argument.

2. Are you a leader or a follower? Use examples and reasons to support your claim.

3. Where you live defines who you are. What is your position? Give examples and reasons to support and develop your opinion.

4. Some prefer to stay home while on vacation while others prefer to travel. Which do you prefer? Why? Give examples and reasons to support your position.

5. Honesty is the best policy. What is your belief? Give illustrations and reasons to support your argument.

6. How do you measure success? Support your position with examples and reasons.

7. Advertising has a positive influence. What is your position? Use examples and reasons to defend your position.

8. Is it better to buy a product when you want it at the regular price or wait for the product when it is on sale? Use examples and reasons to argue your position.

9. In America, customers can return a purchased item for a full refund within thirty days. Do you agree or disagree with this policy? Develop your position with illustrations and reasons.

10. University education should be free. Do you agree or disagree? Why? Use examples and reasons to develop your argument.

11. Laptops should not be permitted in classrooms. What is your position? Give illustrations and reasons to support your opinion.

12. Do you agree or disagree? Every student should travel or work for a year before going to university or college. Support your argument using examples and reasons.

13. It is easy to waste time these days. Do you agree? Give illustrations and reasons to support your opinion.

14. Progress is good. Give illustrations and reasons to support your opinion.

15. Students are less concerned than before. What is your position? Use examples and reasons to defend your argument.

Writing an Objective Essay

As you know, TOEFL uses the independent writing task to measure your ability to write subjectively. TOEFL also measures your ability to write objectively. When you write objectively, you use third person grammar, i.e., "He said...She said...It is...They are...", etc. At an American college or high school, you will also write objective essays. For example, if you are studying psychology, you might write an essay on Sigmund Freud. If you study biology, you might write an essay on bats, etc. The purpose of an objective essay is to inform and educate your audience. You are not trying to persuade them; therefore, do not include your opinion.

Objective Thesis → Informing and Educating

An objective essay starts with an objective thesis or main topic statement. An objective thesis is a fact or general truth that is not arguable, for example:

<u>TOEFL</u> *is an English test.*

<u>Rice</u> *is the most popular food in the world.*

<u>Grizzly bears</u> *are large omnivores.*

Note how the above examples are facts and general truths thus not arguable. Note also how each has a <u>topic</u> and *a controlling idea*, and how each uses third-person (objective) grammar.

- **REMEMBER:** *An objective thesis must be developable, as illustrated below. Greater topic development = a higher score on test day.*

> *TOEFL is an English test.*
>   *or....*
> → *TOEFL is an academic English-language proficiency test comprised of four test sections: reading, listening, speaking, and writing.*

> *Rice is the most popular food in the world.*
>   *or....*
> → *Rice, the most popular food source in the world, can be classified according to grain size.*

> *Grizzly bears are large omnivores.*
>   *or....*
> → *The North American brown bear, or grizzly, is a large omnivore endemic to the mountains of western North America.*

Identifying an Objective Thesis → Rules Checklist

How do you know if what you are writing, or saying, is an objective thesis? Use the rules checklist below. Apply these rules to the following statement to determine if it is an objective thesis or not.

<u>Statement</u>: *India is primarily an agricultural economy in which the three most important crops are rice, wheat, and jowar.*

1) An objective thesis is a fact or general truth. Is this statement a fact or general truth?
   ✓ Yes. India is indeed primarily an agricultural economy in which the three most important crops are in fact rice, wheat, and jowar.

2) An objective thesis has one topic only. Does this statement have one topic?
   ✓ Yes. Topic = "India..."

3) An objective thesis has a topic and a controlling idea. Does this statement have a topic and a controlling idea?
   ✓ Yes. Topic = "India..."; controlling idea = "...is primarily an agricultural economy in which the three most important crops are rice, wheat, and jowar."

4) An objective thesis is supportable. Is this statement supportable? Can it be developed with body paragraph examples?
   ✓ Yes. See the essays on page 64.

5) An objective thesis is a grammatically complete sentence. Is this statement a grammatically complete sentence?
   ✓ Yes. It has a subject ("India...") and a predicate ("...is primarily an agricultural economy in which the three most important crops are rice, wheat, and jowar"). A sentence fragment is not a thesis, i.e.,: *India: A great agricultural economy.*

6) An objective thesis is not a question. Is this statement a question?
   ✓ No. <u>Remember</u>: A thesis is not a question.

7) An objective thesis is not an announcement. Is this statement an announcement?
   ✓ No. "I'm going to write about India's agricultural economy" is an announcement not a thesis. The focus is on the writer's intent not on the thesis.

8) An objective thesis is stated academically, and the controlling idea is developable. Is this statement stated academically? Is the controlling idea developable?
   ✓ Yes. Simply stating a fact, for example, *"India's economy depends on food"* is not a thesis. The topic is clear, yet the controlling idea is not specific enough and limited in scope.

So what is the conclusion? Is the statement an objective thesis? Yes. Why? Because it follows the rules in the objective thesis checklist.

Objective Thesis vs. Subjective Thesis

Look at following examples. Note the contrast between the objective theses (OT = accepted truth/fact, non-opinion) and the subjective theses (ST = opinion).

OT__*A draft is mandatory military service often implemented by governments in times of national crisis.*

ST__Personally, I believe that all young people aged eighteen should be drafted into the military for at least a year.

OT__*Rice, the most popular food source in the world, can be classified according to grain size.*

ST__As far as I'm concerned, Californian rice is better for sushi than Japanese rice.

OT__*The North American brown bear, or grizzly, is a large omnivore endemic to mountains of western North America.*

ST__From my experience, grizzly bears, despite their fearsome reputation, make great pets.

Exercise #24: Thesis Identification → Level 1

Task: Analyze each statement. If it is a subjective thesis, put ST beside it. If it is an objective thesis, put OT. If it is not a thesis, put NT. The answers are on page 202.

_____ 1. Barack Obama is the greatest president in the history of the United States.

_____ 2. Because some people are really stupid.

_____ 3. I love exercising.

_____ 4. Rock and roll is a genre of popular music that originated in the United States after the Second World War.

_____ 5. Hawaii: the best place to go surfing.

_____ 6. To be honest, some people should not do certain stuff.

_____ 7. Personally, I prefer to cook with organic ingredients I grow myself.

_____ 8. Bermuda offers tourists many fun and affordable attractions.

_____ 9. The greatest hero in the history of American sports is Seabiscuit.

_____ 10. In my experience, TOEFL is, for many reasons, far more difficult than IELTS.

_____ 11. A shark is a marine fish with a long body, a cartilaginous skeleton, a dorsal fin, and small rough scales.

_____ 12. Scientists have discovered many things.

_____ 13. Have you ever wondered why you need to drink water?

_____ 14. In my view, we should only work three days a week.

_____ 15. Kind heart, kind person.

Exercise #25: Thesis Identification → Level 2

Task: Analyze each statement. If it is a subjective thesis, put ST beside it. If it is an objective thesis, put OT. If it is not a thesis, put NT. Answers are on page 202.

_____ 1. When Emily was a child, she used to play in the forest near her house where she learned a lot about nature.

_____ 2. Photosynthesis is a critical, life-sustaining process whereby green plants turn light in to chemical energy.

_____ 3. An early form of bridge is the covered bridge and it is important to remember the weather when talking about bridges.

_____ 4. Contrary to popular belief, it was not Columbus but the Vikings who were the first Europeans to set foot on the North American continent.

_____ 5. I really like Star Wars because it has great characters and I really love eating popcorn at the movies.

_____ 6. I contend that city governments should limit development in order to preserve as much open natural space as possible.

_____ 7. Personally speaking, I believe that it is important these days to able to speak not one but two, perhaps even three, languages.

_____ 8. War: Man's worst invention. The solution? Love.

_____ 9. Whales migrate.

_____ 10. As far as I'm concerned, office cubicles are noisy, uncomfortable and, instead of encouraging employee interaction, they make employees irritable and depressed.

_____ 11. The President will be arriving in London today for high-level talks with the British Prime Minister, then he will fly on to Paris and Berlin.

_____ 12. Do you ever wonder how many stars there are in the night sky and if those stars are the same all over the world?

_____ 13. I love the quote, "There's no place like home." It's so true.

_____ 14. It's my belief that the best résumés are simple and to the point while those unlikely to be read are long and full of extraneous details that have no connection to the position in question.

_____ 15. I posit that the job of a scientist is to observe and make conclusions, and have fun teaching students too, if he/she is a professor.

Exercise #26: Thesis Identification → Level 3

Task: Analyze each statement. If it contains a subjective thesis, put ST beside it. If it contains an objective thesis, put OT. If it does contain a thesis, put NT. Check your answers on page 202.

1
2
3
4
5
6
7
8
9
10
11
12
13
14
15
16
17
18
19
20
21
22
23
24
25
26
27
28

_____ 1. After reading Plato—and many, I'm sure, will dispute this assertion—the only conclusion one can draw is that Christianity has borrowed much from that famous Greek philosopher, particularly in regard to knowledge as being a form of light, and light being the symbol of Christ or God.

_____ 2. If history proves one thing it is that kings and tyrants eventually fall and that power, concentrated in the hands of one man, is not permanent but transient in nature, and illusory at best.

_____ 3. A brain drain is defined as a country losing its intellectual capacity due to its citizens migrating to new lands for political and economic reasons, and, by so doing, highlighting the inequities which spurred those moves.

_____ 4. Why, in 1915, was the Sykes-Picot Agreement (also known as the Asia-Minor Agreement) ratified, and why has that singular moment in world history been the cause of so much turmoil in the Middle East since?

_____ 5. Much has been made of the Big Bang Theory, you know, the big cosmic explosion that supposedly heralded the birth of what we call the known universe. But what I really want to share with you today is how I came to love astronomy, then talk about why astronomers the world over need more money for research.

_____ 6. Sir Isaac Newton was a genius, a man, whose inquiry into the laws of the physical world, marks the beginning of the modern era of science, an era that many say ended when Albert Einstein challenged many of Newton's theories, such as mass and energy being interchangeable and not, as Newton postulated, separate and distinct.

29
30
31
32
33
34 _____ 7. A turning point in world history was the battle of the Teutoburg Forest where, in 9 AD, an alliance of Germanic tribes ambushed and destroyed three Roman Legions led by Publius Quinctilius Vara, an action that many historians believe was the beginning of the end of the Roman empire.

35
36
37
38
39 _____ 8. Many ask me what is the secret to success, a question that many a greater mind than mine have asked over the eons without much success; thus it would seem equally futile for me to attempt to define what is essentially undefinable, and therefore move onto the topic of modernity.

40
41
42
43 _____ 9. The passenger pigeon, a bird whose numbers were once so great they blocked out the noon-day sun for hours at a time, was driven into extinction by overhunting and a loss of habitat.

44
45
46
47 _____ 10. A belief system is made up of mutually supportive beliefs. Those beliefs can be classified as religious, philosophical, and ideological, or a combination of each.

48
49
50
51
52
53
54 _____ 11. Violins made by Antonio Stradivari are considered the best in the world. Stradivari was born in Cremona, Italy in 1644. Historians estimate that he made 960 violins and 1,116 other stringed instruments. Of that total, only 640 survive. In 2011, the Lady Blunt Stradivarius, named after Lady Anne Blunt (1837-1917), sold in London for 15.9 million dollars. Suffice it to say, a Stradivarius is worth its weight in gold, and then some.

55
56
57
58
59
60
61 _____ 12. TOEFL is a long and challenging English Test, which consists of four sections: reading, listening, speaking, and writing. On test day, make sure you are prepared. Some students take the test without preparing. As a result, they score low and have to take the test again. A good example is Mario. He took the test and scored low. He then took my TOEFL class. When I met him for the first time, he said, "Wow, TOEFL is really hard."

62
63
64
65
66
67
68
69
70
71
72 _____ 13. Of the fifty states that compromise the Union, a majority are named after Native Americans, such as Alabama, Mississippi, Massachusetts, and Connecticut while others were named by the Spanish, such as Florida and Colorado while New York, New Hampshire, and New Jersey were named by the British to remind them of places back home. California, the most populous state, derives its name from three possible sources. Historians believe that *kali forn* is Native American for "high hills" or possibly the Catalan *calor forn* meaning "hot oven." The third source is the fictional California, a tropical paradise described in the 1590 romance novel *Las Sergas de Esplandian* by Garcia Ordonez de Montalvo.

73
74
75
76 _____ 14. We need to build more zoological gardens inasmuch as they are research laboratories, they support and develop local economies, and they are an ark for those endangered species on the brink of extinction.

77
78 _____ 15. Darwin's theory of evolution remains controversial to this day despite overwhelming evidence to support his claim.

 **Audio Track #5**

Exercise #27: Listening → Thesis Identification

<u>Task</u>: Analyze each statement. If it is a subjective thesis, put ST beside it. If it is an objective thesis, put OT. If it is not a thesis, put NT. Check your answers and the tape script on page 202. The first one has been done for you.

1.   OT

_____

2.

_____

3.

_____

4.

_____

5.

_____

6.

_____

7.

_____

8.

_____

9.

_____

10.

_____

11.

_____

12.

_____

13.

_____

14.

_____

15.

_____

Objective Writing → Short Objective Essay

For TOEFL, you will <u>not</u> write an objective essay; however, you will summarize objective arguments, both verbal and written. To summarize an objective argument proficiently, you must first be able to write an objective essay. By doing so, you will understand how to summarize more proficiently, and score higher on test day.

- **REMEMBER:** *When writing an objective essay, use this three-part structure.*

        1. introduction ⟶ introduces your objective thesis
        2. body ⟶ examples to support your thesis
        3. conclusion ⟶ restates your thesis

Next, let's write a short objective essay. <u>Remember</u>: You are educating your audience. Do not include your opinion.

1	introduction ➜	India is primarily an agricultural economy in which rice is the
2		most important crop.
3		
4	body ➜	In India, the best rice is basmati. Basmati is long and slender,
5		and low in starch. Annually, India produces an average of five-
6		million tons of basmati, 65% of which supplies the world basma-
7		ti market. China and Iran are major importers of Indian basmati
8		with market demand increasing daily. As a result, exporting
9		basmati creates jobs and helps the Indian economy grow.
10		
11	conclusion ➜	In conclusion, basmati rice is the most important crop in India.

- **REMEMBER:** *The essay above is quite short. To develop it, add more examples in the body, as illustrated below. Note para = paragraph.*

1	introduction ➜	India is primarily an agricultural economy in which the three
2		most important crops are rice, wheat, and jowar.
3		
4	body para #1 ➜	In India, the top crop is basmati rice. Basmati is long and slen-
5		der, and low in starch. Annually, India produces an average of
6		five-million tons of basmati, 65% of which supplies the world
7		basmati market. China and Iran are major importers of Indian
8		basmati with market demand increasing daily. By exporting
9		basmati rice, India creates jobs and grows its economy.
10		
11	body para #2 ➜	The next most important crop is wheat. India is the world's sec-
12		ond largest producer of wheat. Wheat is grown primarily in the
13		more temperate north. Every year, Indians consume about 80
14		million tons of wheat with 13 million tons subsidizing sales to
15		the poor. Bread products, such as naan and chapattis, are made
16		from wheat and are the most important food source for India's
17		1.25 billion people. Without wheat, many in India would starve.
18		
19	body para #3 ➜	Finally, there is jowar or sorghum. Jowar is grown in areas
20		which receive less than 100 cms of rainfall a year. Jowar has the
21		same nutritional value as corn. Like corn, jowar is high in starch
22		and is grown primarily to feed livestock and to be made into eth-
23		anol, a gasoline additive. Jowar grows fast and is an important
24		income source for farmers. Because jowar is so versatile and re-
25		silient, both animals and people have come to depend on it.
26		
27	conclusion ➜	In conclusion, India's three most important crops are rice,
28		wheat, and jowar.

Next, let's analyze this objective essay for proficiency.

Question: Does it start with an objective thesis? Answer: Yes. The introduction below contains an objective thesis. It is a fact plus it meets all the requirements of the objective thesis rules checklist on page 57.

introduction ➜ *India is primarily an agricultural economy in which the three most important crops are rice, wheat, and jowar.*

Question: Does the body below support the thesis with enough examples that are well developed? Answer: Yes. The three body paragraphs develop and support the thesis with three distinct examples or supporting topics: *rice, wheat, and jowar.*

1
2
3
4
5
6
7
body para #1 ➜ In India, the top crop is basmati rice. Basmati is long and slender, and low in starch. Annually, India produces an average of five-million tons of basmati, 65% of which supplies the world basmati market. China and Iran are major importers of Indian basmati with market demand increasing daily. **By exporting basmati rice,** *India creates jobs and grows its economy.*

8
9
10
11
12
13
14
15
body para #2 ➜ The next most important crop is wheat. India is the world's second largest producer of wheat. Wheat is grown primarily in the more temperate north. Every year, Indians consume about 80 million tons of wheat with 13 million tons subsidizing sales to the poor. Bread products, such as naan and chapattis, are made from wheat and are the most important food source for India's 1.25 billion people. **Without wheat,** *many in India would starve.*

16
17
18
19
20
21
22
body para #3 ➜ Finally, there is Jowar or sorghum. Jowar is grown in areas which receive less than 100 cms of rainfall a year. Jowar has the same nutritional value as corn. Like corn, jowar is high in starch and is grown primarily to feed livestock and to be made into ethanol, a gasoline additive. Jowar grows fast and is an important income source for farmers. **Because jowar is so versatile and resilient,** *both animals and people have come to depend on it.*

Question: Does each body paragraph give a **cause**-and-*effect* reason that supports the thesis? Answer: Yes. The last sentence in each body paragraph ends with a **cause**-and-*effect* reason that develops and supports the thesis.

Question: Does the conclusion restate the thesis in the introduction? Answer: Yes.

conclusion ➜ In conclusion, India's three most important crops are rice, wheat, and jowar.

As you can see, this objective essay is doing everything right. In other words, it is proficient. Proficient means the writer has demonstrated skill and knowledge when writing an objective essay. By so doing, we (the audience) have learned about India.

Exercise #28: Writing a Short Objective Essay

Task: Choose a topic and write a short objective essay like the one on page 64. You might have to do a little research. Do not time yourself. Just practice writing objectively. Use the eight rhetorical strategies to develop each topic.

1. Steve Jobs
2. pasta
3. Beethoven
4. smartphones
5. chocolate
6. Lady Diana
7. holidays

8. Walt Disney
9. Amazon
10. Titanic
11. Google
12. Elon Musk
13. Paris
14. tennis

15. diamonds
16. soccer
17. Harvard
18. Mars
19. rhinos
20. Nikola Tesla
21. influenza

Notes

Summary Writing → Rhetorical Strategies

For TOEFL, you will not write an objective essay. However, you will summarize objective and subjective arguments in writing and when speaking. Before you summarize, analyze the argument. Identify the rhetorical strategies used to develop the argument. Look at the India essay on page 64. Note how it mainly uses the rhetorical strategies of illustration, description, and cause-and-effect. Next, look at a summary of the same essay below. Note how it restates the thesis and the most important ideas. Both are developed with the same rhetorical strategies used in the essay: illustration, description, and **cause**-and-*effect* reasons.

1 The most important crops in India are rice, wheat, and jowar. The top crop is bas-
2 mati rice. Annually, five million tons are grown. Most is exported to China and
3 Iran. **This** <u>creates jobs and grows the economy</u>. Next is wheat. India is the world's
4 second largest grower. Bread made from wheat is the most important food source
5 in India. **Without it**, <u>many would starve</u>. Jowar (sorghum) grows in harsh envi-
6 ronments and has many uses, such as food for animals and ethanol. Like corn, it
7 is high in starch. **Because it is versatile and resilient**, <u>people and animals de-</u>
8 <u>pend on it</u>.

Next, read the short objective argument below. Note the use of narration, description, illustration, and cause-and-effect.

1 Prohibition was a government ban on the sale, production, importation, and trans-
2 portation of alcohol in the United States from 1920-1933. It was spearheaded by
3 the Anti-Saloon league and the Woman's Christian Temperance Movement. The
4 Volstead Act, the legislation enacting prohibition, was supposed to help cleanse so-
5 ciety of the evils of alcohol; however, in cities like Chicago and New York, it was
6 business as usual with bootlegged alcohol freely flowing from some of the most in-
7 famous gangsters in American history: Alphonse "Al" Capone, Arnold "The Brain"
8 Rothstein, Charles "Lucky" Luciano, and Joseph F. Kennedy, father of assassinated
9 president John F. Kennedy. In 1933, the Volstead Act was repealed and Americans
10 could freely consume alcohol once again.

- **REMEMBER:** *The rhetorical strategies used in the argument to be summarized should also be used in the summary itself, such as below.*

From 1920-1933, the Volstead Act banned alcohol in the United States. This law was supposed to free society from the evils of alcohol. However, gangsters like Al Capone continued to supply alcohol. In 1933, the government ended the ban and people were free to enjoy alcohol once again.

- **REMEMBER:** *When summarizing, do not include all the details. Include only the most important ideas based on the rhetorical strategies used.*

Exercise #29: Summary Writing → Level 1

Task: Read each passage, then summarize it objectively in writing.

1. The Emperor penguin is the largest penguin in the world, standing on average 45 inches tall. To survive the harsh Antarctic winters, they huddle together for warmth. This cooperative behavior is unique in the animal world. The female gives birth to one egg, then leaves it behind with the male as she goes off in search of food. Food is in the ocean, often a 30-mile walk from the rookery.

2. Leonardo Da Vinci was born in the hilltop town of Vinci on April 15, 1452. He was a polymath, a man who was an expert in many different subject areas. Da Vinci is famous for his inventions, such as the flying machine and the parachute. He was a genius far ahead of his time, yet most of his invention never left the drawing board. He never married and died in 1519 at the age of 67.

3. Inventory is a business word that describes the total amount of goods and/or material that a company has on hand. Taking inventory means counting those goods and material. Taking inventory is an essential business practice. Factory owners, for example, need to know how many finished products are available for sale and if they have the material to build more products. Car dealers often have high inventory. To move their old inventory, they often have sales, particularly at the end of the year when new car models are arriving.

4. The hierarchy of Latin honors describes three levels of student achievement. First is cum laude, which means "with honor." Next is magna cum laude. It means "with great honor." The highest honor is summa cum laude. It means "with the highest praise." A "summa" is a student who has demonstrated academic excellence and is at the top of his or her class. Barack Obama graduated magna cum laude from Harvard Law School. Natalie Portman graduated magna cum laude from the University of Pennsylvania while the rapper Ludacris graduated summa cum laude in business from Georgia State University.

5. Tea is the most widely consumed beverage in the world with coffee gaining in popularity. Of the two, tea offers the greatest health benefits. A cup of black tea is filled with anti-oxidants and cancer-fighting compounds, whereas a Harvard study revealed that coffee has no health benefits. Of the two, coffee is higher in caffeine.

6. They are found on every continent but Antarctica and instill fear in many. They can spin silken webs five times stronger than steel. They have eight legs and blue blood. They can grow as wide as eleven inches and as small as the head of a pin. Some are so deadly one bite will kill you while others make excellent pets. Some are considered living fossils while others can run two feet per second. Some give presents while some can jump forty times their body length. Contrary to popular belief, they are not insects, like flies and ants. Instead, they are arachnids or spiders.

Exercise #30: Summary Writing → Level 2

<u>Task</u>: Read each passage, then summarize it objectively in writing.

1. In the early 1960's, many non-native, English speaking students started to apply at American schools. In 1964, the TOEFL paper-based test (PBT) was introduced to assess their English proficiency. TOEFL was developed by the National Council, a cooperative of private and public educational institutions. In 1965, Educational Testing Service (ETS) took over TOEFL. The TOEFL PBT tested reading, listening, and grammar. Speaking and writing were not tested. The early 1980's saw the rise of personal computing. To keep pace with the PC revolution, ETS introduced the TOEFL computer-based test or CBT. The TOEFL CBT tested reading, listening, and grammar. Test-takers also had to write an independent essay. In September 2005, ETS introduced the TOEFL internet-based test or iBT. The TOEFL iBT tests reading, listening, speaking, and writing. The new speaking section replaced the CBT grammar section. Also, the integrated writing task was introduced. That, then, is a short history of TOEFL.

2. Her name was Norma Jeane Baker. The world knew her as the movie star Marilyn Monroe. She was born in Los Angeles on June 1, 1926. As a child, Monroe spent most of her life in foster homes and an orphanage. At sixteen, she married for the first time but divorced soon after. It was then that she changed her name to Marilyn Monroe. During World War II, she worked in a factory where she met a photographer who took photos of her. Hollywood noticed and she soon had small movie roles that led to larger roles in comedies and dramas. By 1953, Monroe, famous for playing "dumb blondes," was starring in such movies as *Niagara, Gentlemen Perform Blondes*, and Billy Wilder's *Some Like it Hot*. Monroe, the most popular sex symbol of the 1950's, married the baseball player Joe DiMaggio, then playwright Arthur Miller. Both marriages ended in divorce. Marilyn Monroe died on August 5, 1962 at the age of 36 having battled depression, addiction, and anxiety all her life. Her last film was *The Misfits* (1961).

3. Before Columbus arrived in 1492, the common belief was that the North American continent was uninhabited, that it truly was virgin territory untouched by mankind. Historians have since dispelled that notion. Contrary to what popular history says, Columbus did not discover North America. North America and the Caribbean, prior to 1492, was populated by numerous indigenous tribes, including hunter-gathers, agriculturalists, and those who harvested the bounty of the oceans. One such tribe was the Arawak of the Bahama Islands. They believed in sharing and did not bear arms. They were hospitable and welcoming. They could spin and weave, and grew corn, yams and cassava. When Columbus set foot on the Bahamas (which he thought was India), his first question to the Arawaks was, "Where is the gold?" Not finding any, Columbus then realized that the Arawaks would "make fine servants." He enslaved fifty and took them back to Europe, most of them perishing on route. This, then, is Columbus' legacy: the start of slavery in the New World.

1   4.   The Singer sewing machine is a little-celebrated technological innovation that
2   revolutionized the lives of American women in the late nineteenth century. By
3   freeing women from the time-consuming labor of making clothes by hand, the
4   Singer sewing machine gave women more time to spend on other chores, pro-
5   vided more free time for themselves, and, perhaps most important of all, al-
6   lowed them to spend their free time getting more politically involved. As a re-
7   sult of increased political activism, women eventually won the right to vote.
8   The Singer Sewing machine: rarely has such a prosaic piece of technology had
9   such an impact on the lives of everyday people.

1   5.   Salmon are a type of fish native to North America. They are andramous, which
2   means they are born in fresh water, migrate to the ocean to grow, then return
3   to their home-river to reproduce and die. An example is the sockeye salmon.
4   After it is born, it spends six months to three years growing in its native river.
5   It is then ready to venture downstream to the ocean, where it will feed for five
6   years. If it survives, it will return to its native river to spawn. On its way, it
7   will face many dangers, such as bears and eagles fattening up for winter.
8   Salmon meat is rich in oil and prized by humans as well.

Notes

_____

_____

_____

_____

_____

_____

_____

_____

_____

_____

_____

_____

_____

_____

_____

_____

_____

_____

Exercise #31: Summary Writing → Level 3

Task: Read each passage, then summarize it objectively in writing.

1. | 1 | The animal kingdom is comprised of cold and warm-blooded animals. The
   | 2 | body temperature of cold-blooded or ectothermic animals is regulated by the
   | 3 | external environment while internal mechanisms keep the body temperature
   | 4 | of warm-blooded or endothermic animals constant. Reptiles, such as lizards
   | 5 | and snakes, are cold-blooded, whereas mammals, such as whales and hu-
   | 6 | mans, are warm-blooded. Most animals are warm-blooded; however, there are
   | 7 | exceptions, such as bats and moles. Their body temperatures vary depending
   | 8 | on whether or not they are active. Because warm-blooded animals generate
   | 9 | body heat internally, they must eat 10 times more than cold-blooded animals.
   | 10 | As a result, warm-blooded animals must be capable of finding food to meet
   | 11 | this need. On the other hand, because cold-blooded animals are heated by the
   | 12 | sun's energy, they require less food.

2. | 1 | When Americans think of a farm, we typically imagine a house and a red barn
   | 2 | with fields full of corn and cows grazing here and there. This type of farm is
   | 3 | called a mixed or family farm. A family farm provides income for the family
   | 4 | while putting food on their table. This was the most common type of farm up
   | 5 | to and just after World War Two. In the late 1950's and early 1960's, commer-
   | 6 | cial farms were supplanting the family farm. A commercial farm specializes in
   | 7 | growing only one crop, called a cash crop, such as corn or soybeans. Often a
   | 8 | corporation will control many commercial farms and produce fruits and vege-
   | 9 | tables on a massive scale. Some farms specialize in raising livestock for mar-
   | 10 | ket. Chicken farms and cattle ranches fall into this category of farm. Fish
   | 11 | farms are also common and supply much of the fresh fish in today's restau-
   | 12 | rants. With the growth of industrial farming, and the demand for fresh organ-
   | 13 | ic produce, many are returning to the family farm as an alternative to mass
   | 14 | produced industrial food products. These days, people are eating healthier. As
   | 15 | a result, they want to know where their food is coming from.

3. | 1 | Cloning is the exact copy of an original organism through asexual reproduc-
   | 2 | tion, using one parent, whereas reproduction consists of two parents, a male
   | 3 | and a female. The most famous cloned animal was Dolly the sheep; however,
   | 4 | Dolly was not an exact replica of her parent. Genetic material from the donor
   | 5 | cell into which Dolly's parent's DNA had be inserted was .01 %. To clone Dol-
   | 6 | ly, it took 277 donor eggs and 29 embryos before birth was achieved. Humans
   | 7 | can be cloned; however, that idea remains controversial. Many believe it is
   | 8 | unethical to harvest human donor eggs and experiment with embryos. Clon-
   | 9 | ing extinct animals, such as the wooly mammoth, however, has gained popu-
   | 10 | larity in recent years. Yet this too has raised serious questions, for bringing
   | 11 | back extinct animals could drastically alter the natural order, particularly an
   | 12 | animal such as the T-Rex.

4. Presidents. What you don't know might surprise you. While on a hunting trip, Theodore Roosevelt (1901-1909) refused to shoot a black bear tied to a tree. He said, "It was unsportsmanlike" and set the bear free. Journalists accompanying the president coined the phrase "teddy bear." James Garfield (1881) was ambidextrous. While writing Greek in his right hand, he could write in Latin in his left. Ulysses S. Grant (1869-1877) got a $20.00 speeding ticket—for riding his horse too fast. Andrew Jackson (1829-1837) had a parrot that loved to curse. During Jackson's funeral, the parrot was swearing so much it had to be removed. James Buchanan (1857-1861) was reportedly gay. Grover Cleveland (1885-1889), before he was president, was a hangman. He also allegedly dated-raped a woman, then had her committed to an insane asylum. Calvin Coolidge (1923-1933) had a pet named Billy. Billy was a pygmy hippopotamus. Dwight Eisenhower (1953-1961), the general who liberated western Europe during World War II, was a gifted painted while Jimmy Carter (1977-1981) is the only president to have seen a UFO. Thomas Jefferson (1801-1809), the writer of the Declaration of Independence, invented the swivel chair while Barack Obama (2008-2016) collects comic books.

5. Celebrating the rites of spring in February dates back to the Romans and the pagan feast of Lupercalia. This pastoral festival celebrated Lupercus, the god of shepherds. It also celebrated Lupa, the she-wolf who nursed the infant orphans, Romulus and Remus, the founders of Rome. The purpose of the festival was to purify new life in spring. Many animals were sacrificed, the blood of which was used to splash on crowds, especially women hoping to ensure fertility and a successful childbirth. Some historians argue that Valentine's Day has its origins in the feast of Lupercalia while others believe that it's named after the Feast of Saint Valentine. Saint Valentine of Rome was imprisoned and eventually executed for performing wedding ceremonies for soldiers not allowed to marry and for spreading Christianity, which had been banned in Rome. According to legend, Valentine healed the daughter of his jailer on the day of his execution, then wrote her a farewell note, signed, "Your Valentine." History records that he was martyred on February 14.

Notes

_____

_____

_____

_____

_____

_____

_____

Speaking Practice

For many test-takers, speaking is a challenge, especially when being timed. Often the pressure is too much. As a result, many blank out. To blank out means your mind goes empty, or blank. You cannot think, so you stop speaking. There are many reasons why you blank out. A big reason is you fear making mistakes thus lack confidence. You can develop confidence when speaking English by first developing your automaticity.

Automaticity → Verbal Brainstorming

Automaticity means you speak English automatically without hesitating or translating. If you pause or hesitate too much when speaking on test day, you will demonstrate a lack of automaticity. This will result in a lower speaking score. The following exercises are designed to help you develop the confidence you need to demonstrate automaticity. They are verbal brainstorming exercises.

Verbal brainstorming starts with a topic, for example hamburger. What do you think when you think of a hamburger? Say whatever you think. Do not worry about making mistakes, just brainstorm, for example:

"Hamburgers, Macdonald's, American culture, popular, I love to make, ketchup, onions, no pickles, hate pickles but love French fries, fries and a burger, love it, yesterday I had a cheeseburger, I'm so hungry!"

Exercise #32: Nouns → Level 1

Task: You have 15 seconds to brainstorm each noun verbally.

1. TOEFL	2. school	3. pen	4. friend
5. pizza	6. car	7. road	8. water
9. doctor	10. candy	11. tea	12. bed
13. phone	14. shoes	15. morning	16. bread

Exercise #33: Nouns → Level 2

Task: You have 15 seconds to brainstorm each noun verbally.

1. weekend	2. lunch	3. map	4. plane
5. computer	6. college	7. parent	8. mountain
9. exam	10. movie	11. holiday	12. present
13. mistake	14. travel	15. dance	16. cook

Exercise #34: Nouns → Level 3

Task: You have 15 seconds to brainstorm each noun verbally.

1. goal	2. psychology	3. issue	4. regret
5. success	6. government	7. border	8. water
9. panda	10. chance	11. security	12. freedom
13. company	14. genius	15. shark	16. advertising

. . . .

Exercise #35: Adjectives → Level 1

Task: You have 15 seconds to brainstorm each adjective verbally.

1. fun	2. hungry	3. sad	4. smart
5. tall	6. hard	7. difficult	8. strong
9. old	10. cute	11. big	12. poor
13. rich	14. red	15. careful	16. boring

Exercise #36: Adjectives → Level 2

Task: You have 15 seconds to brainstorm each adjective verbally.

1. able	2. united	3. emotional	4. traditional
5. responsible	6. successful	7. wise	8. serious
9. significant	10. recent	11. typical	12. accurate
13. foreign	14. global	15. rare	16. pure

Exercise #37: Adjectives → Level 3

Task: You have 15 seconds to brainstorm each adjective verbally.

1. sufficient	2. necessary	3. diligent	4. independent
5. embarrassed	6. beautiful	7. familiar	8. previous
9. aggressive	10. odd	11. willing	12. confident
13. unique	14. frank	15. victorious	16. stubborn

Exercise #38: Adverbs → Level 1

Task: You have 15 seconds to brainstorm each adverb verbally.

1. not	2. always	3. early	4. finally
5. slowly	6. again	7. almost	8. soon
9. never	10. too	11. sometimes	12. really
13. also	14. together	15. often	16. very

Exercise #39: Adverbs → Level 2

Task: You have 15 seconds to brainstorm each adverb verbally.

1. generally	2. quickly	3. exactly	4. especially
5. recently	6. loudly	7. probably	8. already
9. directly	10. mostly	11. usually	12. certainly
13. easily	14. extremely	15. softly	16. daily

Exercise #40: Adverbs → Level 3

Task: You have 15 seconds to brainstorm each adverb verbally.

1. basically	2. currently	3. occasionally	4. primarily
5. firmly	6. ultimately	7. effectively	8. initially
9. essentially	10. lazily	11. eagerly	12. gracefully
13. recklessly	14. skillfully	15. truthfully	16. delicately

. . . .

Exercise #41: Verbs → Level 1

Task: You have 15 seconds to brainstorm each verb verbally.

1. be	2. have	3. do	4. say
5. go	6. get	7. make	8. know
9. think	10. take	11. see	12. come
13. want	14. use	15. give	16. work

Exercise #42: Verbs → Level 2

Task: You have 15 seconds to brainstorm each verb verbally.

1. help	2. believe	3. reach	4. include
5. continue	6. learn	7. understand	8. follow
9. create	10. plan	11. appear	12. build
13. call	14. decide	15. develop	16. delete

Exercise #43: Verbs → Level 3

Task: You have 15 seconds to brainstorm each verb verbally.

1. achieve	2. invest	3. construct	4. hope
5. argue	6. forgive	7. dread	8. consider
9. concentrate	10. debate	11. predict	12. practice
13. rewrite	14. motivate	15. educate	16. procrastinate

. . . .

Exercise #44: Phrasal Verbs → Level 1

Task: You have 15 seconds to brainstorm each phrasal verb verbally.

1. talk about	2. wake up	3. look up	4. try on
5. bring up	6. call back	7. look over	8. know about
9. read about	10. move in	11. switch to	12. clean up
13. work out	14. use up	15. go in	16. try on

Exercise #45: Phrasal Verbs → Level 2

Task: You have 15 seconds to brainstorm each phrasal verb verbally.

1. believe in	2. dream about	3. keep out	4. calm down
5. check out	6. warm up	7. look about	8. turn up
9. dress up	10. go over	11. hold onto	12. let in
13. work out	14. look after	15. hand in	16. check in

Exercise #46: Phrasal Verbs → Level 3

Task: You have 15 seconds to brainstorm each phrasal verb verbally.

1. look up to
2. get away from
3. drop out of
4. look forward to

5. stand up for
6. get through to
7. look around in
8. come down with

9. face up to
10. grow out of
11. watch out for
12. put up with

13. move on to
14. give up on
15. run out of
16. fed up with

Speaking → Rhetorical Strategies

Next, you will practice how to organize your ideas when speaking. You will do so using rhetorical strategies. As you know, rhetorical strategies are tools that help you organize your ideas when speaking. The following exercises will help you do so while helping you develop your automaticity.

Speaking → Definition

Task: For this section, you will define words, such as pen: "A pen is a common writing tool that is long and thin, and filled with ink which is usually black."

Exercise #47: Level 1

Task: You have 15 seconds to define each noun verbally.

1. student
2. rain
3. house
4. tea

5. TOEFL
6. road
7. lion
8. Obama

9. knife
10. October
11. clock
12. apple

13. essay
14. opinion
15. baseball
16. ring

Exercise #48: Level 2

Task: You have 15 seconds to define each noun.

1. fast food
2. nurse
3. park
4. cake

5. hospital
6. son
7. bread
8. bank

9. elephant
10. winter
11. diamond
12. envelope

13. spaghetti
14. Miami
15. cheese
16. husband

Exercise #49: Level 3

<u>Task</u>: You have 15 seconds to define each noun.

1. internet	2. professor	3. proficiency	4. glacier
5. musician	6. sunlight	7. iceberg	8. smartphone
9. microscope	10. First Lady	11. taxi	12. zoo
13. whale	14. T-shirt	15. tsunami	16. beach

Speaking → Illustration + Description

<u>Task</u>: For this section, you will start with a topic noun, such as <u>school</u>. Next, give an example of a school, then describe it. By doing so, you are organizing your ideas by combining the rhetorical strategies of illustration and description, for example:

school: *"An example of a school is my high school in Turkey. It is small. There are about 300 students. It's for boys and girls. It starts at 8 a.m. and ends at 4 p.m. I take the bus to school every day."*

Exercise #50: Level 1

<u>Task</u>: You have 30 seconds to give an example of each noun and describe it.

1. city	2. store	3. friend	4. fruit
5. friend	6. dog	7. test	8. movie
9. vegetable	10. restaurant	11. doctor	12. job
13. pet	14. teacher	15. team	16. candy

Exercise #51: Level 2

<u>Task</u>: You have 30 seconds to give an example of each noun and describe it.

1. sport	2. movie star	3. highway	4. book
5. pasta	6. nut	7. holiday	8. company
9. song	10. island	11. river	12. car
13. dessert	14. problem	15. web site	16. fun

Exercise #52: Level 3

Task: You have 30 seconds to give an example of each noun and describe it.

1. era	2. crime	3. religion	4. ocean
5. museum	6. advice	7. mystery	8. artist
9. medicine	10. law	11. country	12. social media
13. planet	14. invention	15. desert	16. challenge

Speaking → Definition + Illustration + Description

Task: For this section, you will begin with a topic noun, such as <u>airport</u>. Define it, give an example, then describe it. By doing so, you are organizing your ideas by combining the rhetorical strategies of definition, illustration, and description, for example:

airport: *"An airport is a place where airplanes come and go. An example is John F. Kennedy International Airport. It is located in Queens, New York. JFK is about 30 minutes from Manhattan by taxi."*

Exercise #53: Level 1

Task: You have 45 seconds to define each noun, give an example, then describe it.

1. salad	2. actor	3. apartment	4. magazine
5. house	6. meeting	7. juice	8. facebook
9. noise	10. uncle	11. race	12. loan
13. expert	14. dentist	15. salary	16. closet

Exercise #54: Level 2

Task: You have 45 seconds to define each noun, give an example, then describe it.

1. milk	2. opinion	3. mirror	4. staff
5. exit	6. customer	7. hospital	8. novel
9. chicken	10. author	11. career	12. poet
13. stranger	14. farm	15. rent	16. skill

Exercise #55: Level 3

Task: You have 45 seconds to define each noun, give an example, then describe it.

1. concept	2. ambition	3. opportunity	4. independence
5. prayer	6. payment	7. stress	8. interview
9. promotion	10. courage	11. virus	12. option
13. belief	14. injury	15. phobia	16. anxiety

Speaking → Compare-and-Contrast

Task: For this section, you will contrast two ideas, such as <u>fun vs. boring</u>. Define each idea, give an illustration of each, then compare-and-contrast them. By doing so, you are organizing your ideas by combining the rhetorical strategies of definition, illustration, description, and compare-and-contrast, for example:

<u>fun vs. boring</u>: *"Something fun is something you like to do, whereas something boring is something you don't like to do. Playing video games is fun. My favorite is Tetris. However, cleaning my room is boring. I hate dusting and vacuuming."*

- **REMEMBER:** *When you compare-and-contrast, use the following conjunctions.*

  <u>When contrasting...</u>   in contrast, but, however, although, though, even though even if, whereas, yet, still, nevertheless, nonetheless...

  <u>When comparing...</u>   and, also, in addition, moreover, further, besides, plus too, like, just like, much as, much like...

Exercise #56: Level 1

Task: You have 60 seconds to define each pair of ideas, give an example of each, then compare them.

1. breakfast vs. lunch	2. easy vs. hard	3. city vs. country
4. old vs. young	5. happy vs. sad	6. summer vs. winter
7. rich vs. poor	8. friend vs. boss	9. new vs. old
10. student vs. teacher	11. day vs. night	12. laptop vs. desktop

Exercise #57: Level 2

Task: You have 60 seconds to define each pair of ideas, give an example of each, then compare them.

1. mother vs. father	2. cold vs. hot	3. street vs. highway
4. kitchen vs. bedroom	5. hamburger vs. pizza	6. yes vs. no
7. horse vs. cow	8. apple vs. banana	9. dream vs. nightmare
10. dry vs. wet	11. juice vs. alcohol	12. book vs. tablet

Exercise #58: Level 3

Task: You have 60 seconds to define each pair of ideas, give an example of each, then compare them.

1. hope vs. despair	2. pride vs. shame	3. love vs. infatuation
4. safe vs. dangerous	5. jungle vs. desert	6. country vs. continent
7. problem vs. solution	8. soft vs. rough	9. stress vs. relaxation
10. sweet vs. spicy	11. best vs. worst	12. moral vs. immoral

Speaking → Cause-and-Effect → Reasons

Task: For this section, give as many causes as you can for <u>one</u> effect, for example: *"When I eat chocolate, I <u>smile</u>. I also <u>smile</u> when I see a baby and after I finish a good meal. I always <u>smile</u> when I finish work."*

- **REMEMBER:** *A common way to express cause-and-effect is with conditionals.*

  conditional #1   If I eat chocolate (cause), I will smile (effect).

  conditional #2   If I had chocolate (cause), I would smile (effect).

  conditional #3   If I had had chocolate (cause), I would have smiled (effect).

  conditional #4   If I were eating chocolate (cause), I would be smiling (effect).

  conditional #5   If I had been eating chocolate (cause), I would have been smiling (effect).

  conditional #6   If I had eaten chocolate (cause), I would have smiled (effect).

Exercise #59: Level 1

Task: You have 15 seconds to identify as many causes as you can for each effect.

1. laugh	2. cry	3. fun
4. tired	5. scream	6. lazy
7. run	8. angry	9. excited
10. relaxed	11. confused	12. strong

Exercise #60: Level 2

Task: You have 30 seconds to identify as many causes as you can for each effect.

1. alone	2. wonder	3. disappointed
4. sneeze	5. sick	6. realize
7. confident	8. embarrassed	9. hopeful
10. headache	11. inspired	12. thirsty

Exercise #61: Level 3

Task: You have 60 seconds to identify as many causes as you can for each effect.

1. worry	2. trust	3. slow down
4. sympathy	5. motivated	6. depressed
7. suspicious	8. hurry	9. exasperated
10. jealous	11. relieved	12. proud

Speaking → Narration

Task: For this section, you will use the rhetorical strategy of narration to put events in a time order. As you speak, describe each event and give examples. Also, try and use compare-and-contrast, definition, and cause-and-effect. For example, below is a list of words to combine using narration. The response follows.

1. cat	2. dog	3. store
4. friend	5. shy	6. old
7. car	8. shock	9. expensive

Response: *Yesterday, I visited my friend. He has a brown dog named Bob and an orange cat named Bill. The cat was very friendly, but the dog was really shy. My friend and I went shopping in my friend's new car. We went to a big pct store. Pet toys are so expensive. I was shocked. When I got home, I gave my dog dinner. His name is Barley. He is ten-years old.*

Exercise #62: Level 1

Task: You have 30 seconds to use narration and other rhetorical strategies to tell a story using as many of the following words as possible.

1. test	2. TOEFL	3. pay
4. score	5. practice	6. vocabulary
7. goal	8. college	9. register

Exercise #63: Level 2

Task: You have 45 seconds to use narration and other rhetorical strategies to tell a story using as many of the following words as possible.

1. accident	2. police	3. road
4. traffic	5. rain	6. night
7. dangerous	8. fast	9. hospital

Exercise #64: Level 3

Task: You have 60 seconds to use narration and other rhetorical strategies to tell a story using as many of the following words as possible.

1. Apple	2. trailblazer	3. mercurial
4. iPhone	5. Bill Gates	6. drop out
7. internet	8. innovative	9. Steve Jobs

Speaking → Stating a Subjective Verbal Opinion

For this section, you will practice stating subjective verbal opinions. Do so by stating your opinion in one sentence using first-person grammar. For example, state your opinion on the topic of reading books.

Opinion: *Personally, I enjoy reading books.*

- **REMEMBER:** *Use these signal phrases when stating your opinion.*

  In my opinion...   *As far as I'm concerned...*   *In my experience...*
  In my estimation...   *As far as I believe...*   *From my perspective...*
  Personally speaking...   *Basically, I contend that...*   *In the final analysis....*

- **REMEMBER:** *For added practice, state your opinion on each topic in the exercises below. When you are finished one topic, do the next and the next until the end without pausing. This is an excellent automaticity exercise.*

- **REMEMBER:** *Being able to state a subjective verbal opinion proficiently is important for a TOEFL class and on test day.*

- **REMEMBER:** *Make sure your opinions follow the rules checklist on page 71.*

Exercise #65 → Level 1

Task: You have 15 seconds to state a subjective verbal opinion on each topic.

1. cooking	2. shopping	3. Apple
4. homework	5. fast food	6. TOEFL
7. dancing	8. family	9. spicy food
10. work	11. rain	12. texting

Exercise #66 → Level 2

Task: You have 15 seconds to state a subjective verbal opinion on each topic.

1. dating	2. dieting	3. Vincent Van Gogh
4. rap music	5. alcohol	6. angels
7. fish	8. failure	9. pollution
10. fur	11. ballet	12. grades

Exercise #67 → Level 3

Task: You have 15 seconds to state a subjective verbal opinion on each topic.

1. urban living	2. global warming	3. computer games
4. single-parenting	5. volunteering	6. capital punishment
7. abortion	8. euthanasia	9. nuclear weapons
10. refugees	11. sacrificing	12. GM foods

Speaking → Subjective Verbal Opinion + Reason

For this section, you will practice developing a subjective verbal opinion supported by a **cause**-and-*effect* reason. Do so by developing the opinions you stated in the previous three exercises, for example, the topic is reading books.

Opinion-Reason: Personally, **I enjoy reading books** *because I love to learn about people and ideas*.

Exercise #68 → Level 1

Task: You have 30 seconds to state a subjective verbal opinion and develop it with a supporting reason. You have 15 seconds to prepare.

1. cooking	2. shopping	3. Apple
4. homework	5. fast food	6. TOEFL
7. milk	8. family	9. spicy food
10. work	11. rain	12. texting

Exercise #69 → Level 2

Task: You have 30 seconds to state a subjective verbal opinion and develop it with a supporting reason. You have 15 seconds to prepare.

1. dating	2. dieting	3. Vincent Van Gogh
4. rap music	5. alcohol	6. angels
7. fish	8. failure	9. gifts
10. fur	11. ballet	12. grades

Exercise #70 → Level 3

Task: You have 30 seconds to state a subjective verbal opinion and develop it with a supporting reason. You have 15 seconds to prepare.

1. urban living	2. global warming	3. computer games
4. single-parenting	5. volunteering	6. capital punishment
7. abortion	8. euthanasia	9. nuclear weapons
10. refugees	11. sacrificing	12. GM foods

Speaking → Short Subjective Verbal Argument

For this section, you will develop short subjective verbal arguments for each previous topic. Your argument should contain a **cause-and-effect opinion**, *an example*, and end with *a conclusion with a cause-and-effect reason*, for example:

Argument: **Personally, I enjoy reading books because I love to learn about people and ideas.** *For example, I am now reading a book about ancient Rome. I am learning about the architecture, such as the Coliseum, and about people like Caesar.* <u>*By doing so, I will know about Rome when I go there next summer for a vacation.*</u>

Exercise #71 → Level 1

Task: You have 45 seconds to state a subjective verbal opinion and develop it with a supporting reason. You have 15 seconds to prepare.

1. cooking	2. shopping	3. Apple
4. homework	5. fast food	6. TOEFL
7. milk	8. family	9. spicy food
10. work	11. rain	12. texting

Exercise #72 → Level 2

Task: You have 45 seconds to state a subjective verbal opinion and develop it with a supporting reason. You have 15 seconds to prepare.

1. dating	2. dieting	3. Vincent Van Gogh
4. rap music	5. alcohol	6. angels
7. fish	8. failure	9. pollution
10. fur	11. ballet	12. grades

<u>Exercise #73</u> → Level 3

<u>Task</u>: You have 60 seconds to develop a short subjective verbal argument for each topic. You have 20 seconds to prepare.

1. urban living   2. global warming   3. computer games

4. single-parenting   5. volunteering   6. capital punishment

7. abortion   8. euthanasia   9. nuclear weapons

10. refugees   11. sacrificing   12. GM foods

<u>Topic Development</u> → The Five W's

When you develop a sentence, a paragraph, or an argument, you are adding details to develop the topic. This section will help you practice topic development. Do so by using the five W's: *Who, What, Where, When, Why, and How.* Look at the sample sentence below. It clearly lacks development. Let's develop it using the five W's.

Sample: *David and Susan bought a house.*

1. <u>Who</u> are they?

   David and Susan <u>Morgan</u> bought a house.

2. <u>What</u> is their marital status?

   <u>Newlyweds</u> David and Susan Morgan bought a house.

4. <u>What kind</u> of house did they buy?

   Newlyweds David and Susan Morgan bought a <u>new</u> house.

5. <u>Where</u> did they buy their house?

   Newlyweds David and Susan Morgan bought a new house <u>in Westport, Connecticut</u>.

6. <u>When</u> did they buy their house?

   Newlyweds David and Susan Morgan <u>recently</u> bought a new house in Westport, Connecticut.

7. <u>How much</u> did they pay for the house?

   Newlyweds David and Susan Morgan recently bought a new house <u>for an amazingly low price</u> in Westport, Connecticut.

8. <u>Where</u> is Westport, Connecticut?

Newlyweds David and Susan Morgan recently bought a new house for an amazingly low price in Westport, Connecticut, <u>which is a sixty-minute train ride from Grand Central Station in midtown Manhattan</u>.

9. <u>Why</u> did they buy a new house?

Newlyweds David and Susan Morgan recently bought a new house for an amazingly low price in Westport, Connecticut, which is a sixty-minute train ride from Grand Central Station in midtown Manhattan, <u>because they want to raise a family</u>.

- **REMEMBER:** *Greater topic development means a higher score for the speaking and writing sections of TOEFL and IELTS. Topic development is contrasted below. Which sentence do you think would score higher on test day, A or B? B definitely. Why? Greater topic development.*

    A. David and Susan bought a house.

    B. Newlyweds David and Susan Morgan recently bought a new house for an amazingly low price in Westport, Connecticut, which is a sixty-minute train ride from Grand Central Station in midtown Manhattan, because they want to raise a family.

Exercise #74 → Level 1

<u>Task</u>: Develop each sentence using the five W's.

1.   A mosquito is an insect.

2.   Steve Jobs changed the world.

3.   Africa is a big continent.

4.   A car is very useful.

5.   The internet is not always safe.

6.   Dieting is hard.

7.   There are four seasons.

8.   Soccer is a popular sport.

9.   Many don't like going to the dentist.

10.   The Amazon is a big river in Brazil.

11.   Cats and dogs are common pets.

12. Some people don't like red meat.

13. You can do a lot with a smartphone.

14. Amy suffers from food allergies.

15. An app is a useful computer tool.

Exercise #75 → Level 2

Task: Develop each sentence using the five W's. Do research as needed.

1. The first step in looking for a job is identifying the type of job you want.

2. The history of coffee goes back to at least the tenth century.

3. There are many reasons for why the divorce rate is so high worldwide.

4. Young children often copy the behavior of older children.

5. Abraham Lincoln is considered to be the greatest American president.

6. Pasta can be classified according to shape.

7. Making a lot of money is not everyone's goal.

8. There are many types of music, including pop, rock, and rap.

9. Penguins are flightless birds found in Antarctica.

10. Coca-Cola is the world's most popular brand.

11. Multi-tasking means doing many jobs at the same time.

12. One of the most famous disasters in history was the sinking of the *Titanic*.

13. In the not-too-distant future, space tourism will become very popular.

15. If you love sweets, you have "a sweet tooth."

Exercise #76 → Level 3

Task: Develop each sentence using the five W's. Do research as needed.

1. At first, Ryan was very hesitant to call Mary.

2. A whale is not a fish but a mammal.

3. As a result of global warming, scientists predict that ocean levels will rise precipitously in the next one hundred years.

4. Life is full of challenges.

5. Psychology is the study of the human mind and human behavior.

6. The African plain is home to myriad predators, the biggest of which are lions.

7. Man has always pushed the limits of experience in order to test himself and to explore new frontiers.

8. While the internet is fast and convenient, it does have its drawbacks.

9. Defined, gender equality means that both men and women receive equal treatment without discrimination.

10. Bread has been a staple for millions ever since man learned how to harvest and process wheat.

11. Sometimes it is hard to concentrate.

12. Beauty is only skin deep.

13. In the world of computer hacking, there are good guys and bad guys.

14. Many famous people have gone to Stanford University, including Evan Spiegel and Bobby Murphy. And let's not forget Larry Page and Sergey Brin.

15. Veganism is a lifestyle many are pursuing these days for myriad reasons.

16. Wellington and Napoleon met at Waterloo.

17. 3D printing (AM) is a game changer.

18. A unicorn is a mythical animal.

19. The best students are not always the smartest.

20. You must be cruel to be kind.

Speaking → Short Verbal Arguments → More Practice

Task: For this section, you will deliver short, verbal arguments using the strategies previously discussed. Take a position on each topic. Start by stating your opinion, give a *supporting example(s)*, then end with a **cause-and-effect** reason in your conclusion.

- **REMEMBER:** *Develop your supporting examples using the five W's.*

1	Argument:	Personally, I enjoy reading books because I love to learn about people.
2		*For example, I'm now reading a book about Julius Caesar. Before he*
3		*was the Emperor of Rome, he was a great general. He won many bat-*
4		*tles and returned home with his army. However, he had to stop at the*
5		*Rubicon River. Roman law said he could not cross the Rubicon River*
6		*and enter Rome with an army. But he did. Once across the Rubicon Riv-*
7		*er, Caesar and his army entered Rome and freed it from corrupt politi-*
8		*cians. Caesar became emperor and the idiom "to cross the Rubicon"*
9		*was born. It means you have crossed a line and you can't go back. You*
10		*must go forward, no matter what.* As you can see, **by reading, I**
11		**learned a new idiom while learning about Julius Caesar and Rome.**

Exercise #77 → Level 1

Task: You have 45 seconds to develop a short verbal argument for each topic. You have 15 seconds to prepare your response.

1. smoking	2. more homework	3. video games
4. spam	5. flying	6. facebook
7. credit cards	8. tattoos	9. traveling alone
10. jewelry	11. giving a gift	12. taking a bus

Exercise #78 → Level 2

Task: You have 45 seconds to develop a short verbal argument for each topic. You have 15 seconds to prepare your response.

1. bullying	2. school uniforms	3. computers make us lazy
4. driverless cars	5. nose rings	6. no food in movie theatres
7. all raw food diet	8. plastic surgery	9. working while a student
10. internet piracy	11. recycling	12. having a blood test

Exercise #79 → Level 3

Directions: You have 60 seconds to develop a short verbal argument for each topic. You have 20 seconds to prepare your response.

1. studying art	2. girls on boys' teams	3. a license to be a parent
4. colonizing Mars	5. same sex marriages	6. 9 p.m. curfew for teens
7. OK for men to cry	8. Barbie as a role model	9. 2 kids per house max
10. ban all texting	11. adopting a child	12. women in combat

Speaking → Verbal Summaries

When you verbally summarize an argument, paraphrase the most important ideas. Those ideas are based on the rhetorical strategies used, for example, in the sample below, cause-and-effect and illustration are the rhetorical strategies used and repeated in the summary.

Sample: Technology has changed our lives in numerous way. The steam engine led to the first trains, the aqualung allowed us to enter the ocean for extended periods, and the light bulb conquered the night.

Summary: Technology, such as the steam engine, the aqualung, and the light bulb, has changed our lives.

● **REMEMBER:** *For practice, summarize the following exercises in writing as well.*

Exercise #80 → Level 1

Task: You have 30 seconds to read each passage. You have 45 seconds to summarize each verbally.

1. 1. Despite being arid, inhospitable places, deserts are, in fact, home to a wide va-
2.   riety of animal species that have adopted unique survival skills.
3.
4. 2. Bakelite is an early form of plastic originally used to protect hardwood floors,
5.   such as those in bowling alleys. It was created by Dr. Baekeland in Yonkers,
6.   New York in 1910.
7.
8. 3. The Ford Model T, or "Tin Lizzie," was the first mass-produced automobile built
9.   on a production line. The process reduced costs, made cars affordable to all,
10.   and revolutionized the manufacturing process.
11.
12. 4. Plastic surgery is a process in which a doctor alters a person's appearance by
13.   repairing or reconstructing parts of the body. Movie stars are famous for hav-
14.   ing plastic surgery.

15
16
17
18
19
5. In 1886, German inventor Karl Benz patented his "vehicle powered by a gas engine" and gave birth to the automobile. Two years later, in August, 1888, Benz's wife Bertha, along with their two children, used the vehicle to make the world's first long-distance journey by car.

20
21
22
6. Pickling is a method of food preservation that extends the life of food by marinating it in a high-salt solution called brine.

23
24
25
26
7. Do UFO's exist or are they really just figments of our imaginations? Many believe they are real and that we are in fact being visited by extraterrestrials. However, many remain skeptical.

27
28
29
30
31
8. A soothsayer is a person who, by reading omens, practices divination, the predicting of events. A soothsayer is a spiritual guide. The most famous ancient soothsayer was the Oracle of Delphi in Greece. Other names for soothsayers are shamans and witch doctors.

32
33
34
35
36
9. Freckles are dark areas of skin the body creates to protect the skin from ultra-violent light. There are two types of freckles: simple, which are light and appear in childhood, and sunburn freckles, which are a result of prolonged exposure to the sun.

37
38
39
40
10. Roman women wore a long tunic called a stola. Stolas were made of silk and wool, depending on the woman's social position. Roman women also dyed their hair. The most common hair color was golden-red.

41
42
43
44
45
46
11. In America, college sports are big business. Television gives millions to schools for the right to broadcast their games. Coaches too benefit enormously. Some college coaches are multi-millionaires while the players, the stars, the reasons for all that money changing hands, do not get paid. This injustice has not gone unnoticed.

47
48
49
50
51
12. Because of global warming, the ice in the Arctic is rapidly melting and threatening to change forever Inuit culture as we know it. That culture is based on hunting seals and polar bears, animals which need the Arctic ice to survive. When the ice goes, so do the seals, the polar bears, and the Inuit.

52
53
54
55
13. Bullying is the act of using superior force to intimidate a weaker individual, whereas cyberbullying occurs when a child is harassed, embarrassed, or threatened online by another child or preteen.

56
57
58
59
14. A Beefeater is a ceremonial guard assigned to protect the Tower of London in England. Beefeaters are ex-military selected for their conduct and awards of distinction. The order was founded in 1485 under Henry VII.

60
61
62
15. Persepolis, situated sixty kilometers south of the city of Shiraz, was the capital of ancient Iran. This World Heritage Site exists today as ruins, having been destroyed by Alexander the Great in 33 BCE.

Exercise #81 → Level 2

Task: You have 5 minutes to read each passage. You have 60 seconds to summarize each verbally.

1. 1. Prohibition was a government ban on the sale, production, importation, and
2. transportation of alcohol in the United States from 1920-1933. It was spear-
3. headed by the Anti-Saloon league and the Woman's Christian Temperance
4. Movement. The Volstead Act, the legislation enacting prohibition, was sup-
5. posed to help cleanse society of the evils of alcohol; however, in cities like Chi-
6. cago and New York, it was business as usual with bootlegged alcohol freely
7. flowing from some of the most famous gangsters in American history: Al-
8. phonse "Al" Capone, Arnold "The Brain" Rothstein, Charles "Lucky" Luciano,
9. and Joseph F. Kennedy, father of assassinated president John F. Kennedy. In
10. 1933, the Volstead Act was repealed and Americans could freely consume al-
11. cohol once again.

1. 2. History recalls many great leaders, but few as great as Napoleon Bonaparte.
2. He was born on August 15, 1769 on the island of Corsica. After attending mil-
3. itary school, he fought with distinction in the French Revolution of 1789. He
4. rose through the ranks and won many famous battles. In 1804, he crowned
5. himself Emperor of France with much of Europe under his rule. As emperor
6. he reshaped the French legal system. He centralized the government, made
7. education more available to the middle class, and introduced the Napoleonic
8. Code, a series of laws that introduced freedom of religion, equality before the
9. law, the abolition of serfdom, and the protection of property rights. Fearing
10. Russia, he invaded yet was defeated at the gates of Moscow. With Europe
11. against him, he abdicated and was sent into exile on the island of Elba, from
12. which he escaped and returned to France, intent on restoring the empire he
13. lost. However, it was not to be. On June 18, 1815 he was defeated by a com-
14. bined Anglo-Dutch and Prussian army under the Duke of Wellington at the
15. Battle of Waterloo. Once again Napoleon was sent into exile, this time to the
16. remote island of St. Helena in the South Atlantic, where he died on May 5,
17. 1821. Tyrant or hero, there is no denying Napoleon Bonaparte's place in his-
18. tory.

3. Before Columbus arrived in 1492, the common belief was that the North
American continent was uninhabited, that it truly was virgin territory untouched by mankind. Historians have since dispelled that notion. Contrary to
what popular history says, Columbus did not discover North America. North
America and the Caribbean, prior to 1492, were populated by numerous indigenous tribes, including hunter-gathers, agriculturists, and those who harvested the oceans. One such tribe was the Arawak of the Bahama Islands.
They believed in sharing and did not bear arms. They were hospitable and
welcoming. They could spin and weave, and grew corn, yams, and cassava.
When Columbus set foot on the Bahamas (which he thought was India), his
first question to the Arawaks was, "Where is the gold?" Not finding any, Columbus then realized that the Arawaks would "make fine servants." He enslaved fifty and took them back to Europe, most of them perishing on route.
This, then, is Columbus' legacy: the start of slavery in the New World.

4. The Singer sewing machine is a little-celebrated technological innovation that revolutionized the lives of American women in the late nineteenth century. By freeing women from the time-consuming labor of making clothes by hand, the Singer sewing machine gave women more time to spend on other chores, provided more free time for themselves, and, perhaps most important of all, allowed them to spend their free time getting more politically involved. As a result of increased political activism, women eventually won the right to vote. The Singer Sewing machine: rarely has such a prosaic piece of technology had such an impact on the lives of everyday people.

5. Celebrating the rites of spring in February dates back to the Romans and the pagan feast of Lupercalia. This pastoral festival celebrated Lupercus, the god of shepherds. It also celebrated Lupa, the she-wolf who nursed the infant orphans, Romulus and Remus, the founders of Rome. The purpose of the festival was to to purify new life in spring. Many animals were sacrificed, the blood of which was used to splash on crowds, especially women hoping to ensure fertility and a successful childbirth. Some historians argue that Valentine's Day has its origins in the feast of Lupercalia while others believe that is it named after the Feast of Saint Valentine. Saint Valentine of Rome was imprisoned and eventually executed for performing wedding ceremonies for soldiers not allowed to marry, and for spreading Christianity, which had been banned in Rome. According to legend, Valentine healed the daughter of his jailer on the day of his execution, then wrote her a farewell note signed, "Your Valentine." History records that he was martyred on February 14.

6. Presidents. What you don't know might surprise you. While on a hunting trip, Theodore Roosevelt (1901-1909) refused to shoot a black bear tied to a tree. He said, "It was unsportsmanlike" and set the bear free. Journalists accompanying the president coined the phrase "teddy bear." James Garfield (1881) was ambidextrous. While writing Greek in his right hand, he could write in Latin in his left. Ulysses S. Grant (1869-1877) got a $20.00 speeding ticket— for riding his horse too fast. Andrew Jackson (1829-1837) had a parrot that loved to curse. During Jackson's funeral, the parrot was swearing so much it had to be removed. James Buchanan (1857-1861) was reportedly gay. Grover Cleveland (1885-1889), before he was president, was a hangman. He also allegedly dated-raped a woman, then had her committed to an insane asylum. Calvin Coolidge (1923-1933) had a pet named Billy. Billy was a pygmy hippopotamus. Dwight Eisenhower (1953-1961), the general who liberated western Europe during World War II, was a gifted painted while Jimmy Carter (1977-1981) is the only president to have seen a UFO. Thomas Jefferson (1801-1809), the writer of the Declaration of Independence, invented the swivel chair while Barack Obama (2009-2017) collects comic books.

7. Salmon are a type of fish native to North America. They are andramous, which means they are born in fresh water, migrate to the ocean to grow, then return to their home-river to reproduce and die. An example is the sockeye salmon. After it is born, it spends six months to three years growing in its native river. It is then ready to venture downstream to the ocean, where it will feed for five years. If it survives, it will return to its native river to spawn. On its way, it

7   will face many dangers, such as bears and eagles fattening up for winter.
8   Salmon meat is rich in oil and prized by humans as well.

1   8.   DDT is a controversial insecticide. It is a tasteless, odorless, crystalline orga-
2   nohchloride that is a highly effective insecticide. During World War Two, DDT
3   was introduced as a means of controlling typhus and malaria among troops
4   and civilians. It was so effective that after the war, it was used as a highly ef-
5   fective agricultural pesticide and is credited with controlling malaria in high-
6   risk areas. Paul Hermann Muller, the Swiss chemist who identified DDT's in-
7   secticidal properties, was awarded the Nobel Prize in 1948 for his work. How-
8   ever, in 1962, author Rachel Carson, in her book *Silent Spring*, described how
9   DDT was destroying the environment. Carson showed how DDT was causing
10   cancer in people and endangering many animals, particularly birds, such as
11   falcons and eagles. As a result, in 1972, DDT was banned in the United States
12   and was later banned worldwide. DDT is still used today to control disease
13   vectors in high-risk areas, a practice the remains controversial despite the
14   health benefits.

1   9.   When Americans think of a farm, we typically imagine a house and a red barn
2   with fields full of corn and cows grazing here and there. This type of farm is
3   called a mixed or family farm. A family farm provides income for the family
4   while putting food on their table. This was the most common type of farm up
5   to and just after World War Two. In the late 1950's and early 1960's, commer-
6   cial farms were supplanting the family farm. A commercial farm specializes in
7   growing only one crop, called a cash crop, such as corn or soybeans. Often a
8   corporation will control many commercial farms and produce fruits and vege-
9   tables on a massive scale. Some farms specialize in raising livestock for mar-
10   ket. Chicken farms and cattle ranches fall into this category of farm. Fish
11   farms are also common in many countries and supply much of the fresh fish
12   in restaurants today. With the growth of industrial farming, and the demand
13   for fresh organic produce, many are returning to the family farm as an alter-
14   native to mass produced industrial food products. These days, people are eat-
15   ing healthier. As a result, they want to know where their food is coming from.

1   10. In the early 1960's, many non-native, English-speaking students started to
2   apply at American schools. In 1964, the TOEFL paper-based test (PBT) was
3   introduced to assess their English proficiency. TOEFL was developed by the
4   National Council, a cooperative of private and public educational institutions.
5   In 1965, ETS took over TOEFL. The TOEFL PBT tested reading, listening and
6   grammar. Speaking and writing were not tested. The early 1980's saw the rise
7   of personal computing. To keep pace with the PC revolution, ETS introduced
8   the TOEFL computer-based test or CBT. The TOEFL CBT tested reading, lis-
9   tening, and grammar. Test-takers also had to write an independent essay. In
10   September 2005, ETS introduced the TOEFL internet-based test or iBT. The
11   TOEFL iBT tests reading, listening, speaking and writing. The speaking sec-
12   tion replaced the CBT grammar section. Also, the integrated writing task was
13   introduced. That, then, is a short history of TOEFL.

Exercise #82 → Level 3

<u>Task</u>: You have 10 minutes to read the following passage by Frederick Douglas (1818-1895). You have 60 seconds to summarize it.

1　"I was born in Tuckahoe, near Hillsborough, and about twelve miles from
2　Easton, in Talbot county, Maryland. I have no accurate knowledge of my age, never
3　having seen any authentic record containing it. By far the larger part of the slaves
4　know as little of their ages as horses know of theirs, and it is the wish of most mas-
5　ters within my knowledge to keep their slaves thus ignorant. I do not remember to
6　have ever met a slave who could tell of his birthday. They seldom come nearer to it
7　than planting-time, harvest-time, cherry-time, spring-time, or fall-time. A want of
8　information concerning my own was a source of unhappiness to me even during
9　childhood. The white children could tell their ages. I could not tell why I ought to
10　be deprived of the same privilege. I was not allowed to make any inquiries of my
11　master concerning it. He deemed all such inquiries on the part of a slave improper
12　and impertinent, and evidence of a restless spirit. The nearest estimate I can give
13　makes me now between twenty-seven and twenty-eight years of age. I come to this,
14　from hearing my master say, sometime during 1835, I was about seventeen years
15　old.

16　My mother was named Harriet Bailey. She was the daughter of Isaac and Betsey
17　Bailey, both colored, and quite dark. My mother was of a darker complexion than
18　either my grandmother or grandfather.

19　My father was a white man. He was admitted to be such by all I ever heard speak
20　of my parentage. The opinion was also whispered that my master was my father;
21　but of the correctness of this opinion, I know nothing; the means of knowing was
22　withheld from me. My mother and I were separated when I was but an infant—
23　before I knew her as my mother. It is a common custom, in the part of Maryland
24　from which I ran away, to part children from their mothers at a very early age. Fre-
25　quently, before the child has reached its twelfth month, its mother is taken from it,
26　and hired out on some farm a considerable distance off, and the child is placed
27　under the care of an old woman, too old for field labor. For what this separation is
28　done, I do not know, unless it be to hinder the development of the child's affection
29　toward its mother, and to blunt and destroy the natural affection of the mother for
30　the child. This is the inevitable result.

31　I never saw my mother, to know her as such, more than four or five times in my
32　life; and each of these times was very short in duration, and at night. She was
33　hired by a Mr. Stewart, who lived about twelve miles from my home. She made her
34　journeys to see me in the night, travelling the whole distance on foot, after the per-
35　formance of her day's work. She was a field hand, and a whipping is the penalty of
36　not being in the field at sunrise, unless a slave has special permission from his or
37　her master to the contrary—a permission which they seldom get, and one that
38　gives to him that gives it the proud name of being a kind master. I do not recollect
39　of ever seeing my mother by the light of day. She was with me in the night. She
40　would lie down with me, and get me to sleep, but long before I waked she was gone.
41　Very little communication ever took place between us. Death soon ended what little
42　we could have while she lived, and with it her hardships and suffering. She died
43　when I was about seven years old, on one of my master's farms, near Lee's Mill

Part II

Academic English Practice

Structure → Exercise #1

Task: Fill in the blanks with the correct words. Check your answers on page 203.

1. TOEFL _____ four hours long.

        a. is
        b. a
        c. an
        d. the

2. TOEFL is an English language _____ test.

        a. proficiently
        b. proficiency
        c. professional
        d. prolific

3. Pierre _____ Susie to teach him TOEFL.

        a. need
        b. see
        c. is
        d. wants

4. Last night, Brunna _____ a new strategy in her TOEFL class.

        a. learned
        b. borrowed
        c. found
        d. caught

5. Anna asked her TOEFL teacher _____ help with the reading section.

        a. of
        b. at
        c. on
        d. for

6. Marjan loves to study TOEFL, _____ Farshad hates it.

        a. and
        b. but
        c. also
        d. moreover

7.   TOEFL consists _____ four sections: reading, listening, speaking, and writing.

        a. in
        b. of
        c. at
        d. an

8.   Your TOEFL score is _____ total of 120 points.

        a. an
        b. at
        c. a
        d. the

9.   To get a high TOEFL score, you _____ study a lot.

        a. able
        b. must
        c. could
        d. will

10. The average worldwide TOEFL score in 2016 _____ 81/120.

        a. were
        b. has been
        c. was
        d. had been

11. If you take a TOEFL class, you _____ learn strategies from the instructor.

        a. would
        b. will
        c. might
        d. are

12. TOEFL is scored from 0 _____ 120.

        a. and
        b. to
        c. up
        d. between

Written Expression → Exercise #1

Task: Identify the error in each passage. Check your answers on page 203.

1. To prepare for the TOEFL test, <u>many</u> test-takers <u>will take</u> a TOEFL class two
                                         A   B

   <u>and</u> three times in order to be test ready <u>on</u> test day.
   C   D

2. The <u>firstly</u> TOEFL test was <u>called</u> the TOEFL PBT (paper-based <u>test</u>). It was fol-
         A   B   C

   lowed <u>by</u> the TOEFL CBT (computer-based test) and the TOEFL iBT (internet-
         D

   based test).

3. <u>Some</u> test-takers prefer to prepare <u>for</u> TOEFL alone <u>while</u> others prefer to take
   A   B   C

   <u>the</u> class.
   D

4. Before she <u>took</u> the TOEFL test, Julia <u>takes</u> three TOEFL classes and <u>bought</u>
             A   B   C

   four TOEFL <u>texts</u>.
             D

5. <u>For</u> each reading section passage, you will answer <u>between</u> 12 and 14 multiple-
   A   B

   <u>choice</u> questions, five <u>which</u> are vocabulary questions.
   C   D

6. If you are not happy <u>for</u> your TOEFL score, you can <u>retake</u> the test <u>as many</u>
                          A   B   C

   times <u>as you wish</u>.
          D

7. <u>Your</u> TOEFL score <u>is good for two years</u>. After that, you <u>must</u> renew it by
   A   B   C

   <u>retake the test</u>.
      D

8. Your passport <u>it</u> is your <u>best form</u> of <u>identification</u> <u>on</u> test day.
                A   B   C   D

9. <u>Defined</u>, <u>proficiency</u> means theory <u>and</u> knowledge applied <u>on</u> practice.
   A   B   C   D

10. Diligence <u>and</u> persistence <u>are</u> the secret <u>to</u> TOEFL <u>succeeding</u>.
           A   B   C   D

11. <u>If you think</u> you got <u>a higher writing or speaking score</u>, you <u>can ask ETS</u>
     A   B   C
<u>rescore your response</u>.
        D

12. <u>By test day</u>, before you take the test, you will do <u>a sound check</u> to make sure
      A   B
that your <u>headset</u> is <u>working properly</u>.
           C   D

13. Olga <u>took the TOEFL</u> test <u>ten time</u> before <u>she</u> finally got the score she <u>needed</u>.
         A   B   C   D

14. <u>After</u> the listening <u>section</u>, there <u>is</u> a ten-minute <u>brake</u>.
    A   B   C   D

15. <u>You</u> must <u>register</u> <u>to</u> the TOEFL test <u>online</u>.
    A   B   C   D

16. The best <u>resourse</u> <u>for</u> TOEFL information <u>is</u> ETS's <u>website</u>, www.ets.org/toefl.
          A   B   C   D

17. <u>TOEFL can test</u> your <u>ability to manage</u> your time <u>when</u> answering <u>questions</u>.
      A   B   C   D

18. <u>Do</u> you know <u>anybody</u> <u>whose</u> taken <u>the TOEFL test</u>?
    A   B   C   D

19. <u>Many</u> test-takers <u>want</u> a TOEFL score to put <u>in</u> their <u>résumés</u>.
     A   B   C   D

20. <u>Test-ready</u> means you are <u>prepared</u> <u>to</u> take <u>a</u> TOEFL test.
      A   B   C   D

21. <u>On test day</u>, when you write <u>your independant essay</u>, you will <u>see a word</u>
      A   B   C
counter <u>on your computer screen</u>.
             D

22. <u>Ten business days after you take the TOEFL test</u>, you will receive your unoffi-
                        A
cial TOEFL score <u>by regular mail</u>. If you want to send your score <u>to the</u>
                    B   C
<u>school as part of your application package</u>, you must ask ETS to send your
official score directly <u>to the school for a fee</u>.
                              D

<u>Vocabulary</u> → **Exercise #1**

<u>Task</u>: Choose the correct synonym. Check your answers on page 204.

1. thesis (n)

    a. claim
    b. essay
    c. system
    d. knowledge

2. proficiency (n)

    a. skill and knowledge
    b. skill and essays
    c. skill and language
    d. skill and luck

3. arduous (adj)

    a. difficult
    b. silly
    c. fun
    d. interesting

4. example (n)

    a. piece
    b. part
    c. illustration
    d. idea

5. paraphrase (v)

    a. perform
    b. repeat
    c. rewrite
    d. restate

6. scrutinize (v)

    a. examine often
    b. examine briefly
    c. examine closely
    d. examine rarely

7. essay (n)

    a. verbal thesis
    b. written idea
    c. new argument
    d. written argument

8. topic (n)

    a. story
    b. example
    c. subject
    d. theme

9. ascertain (v)

    a. make sure of
    b. make fun of
    c. make little of
    d. make plain

10. subjective (adj)

    a. personal
    b. objective
    c. accurate
    d. ideas

11. tranquil (adj)

    a. peaceful
    b. noisy
    c. tenuous
    d. predictable

12. rewrite (v)

    a. redo
    b. resend
    c. return
    d. repeat

13. ambiguous (adj)

    a. not right
    b. not clear
    c. not smart
    d. not nice

14. erroneous (adj)

    a. dangerous
    b. believable
    c. correct
    d. mistaken

15. drop out of (v)

    a. leave
    b. return
    c. fail
    d. deliver

16. feasible (adj)

    a. possible
    b. probable
    c. proficient
    d. effective

17. inasmuch as (adv)

    a. totally
    b. maybe
    c. already
    d. because

18. formidable (adj)

    a. challenging
    b. threatening
    c. worrying
    d. formulaic

<u>Structure</u> → **Exercise #2**

<u>Task</u>: Fill in the blanks with the correct words. Check your answers on page 204.

1. On test day, each test-taker will _____ note paper and pencils.

        a. be given
        b. be supplying
        c. be supplied
        d. be helped with

2. TOEFL's _____ competitor is IELTS.

        a. testing
        b. England
        c. competing
        d. British

3. On test day, _____ your passport to the test center for identification.

        a. took
        b. take
        c. taken
        d. gave

4. TOEFL is designed and implemented _____ Educational Testing Service (ETS).

        a. in
        b. for
        c. by
        d. on

5. The _____ challenging section on the TOEFL test is the reading section.

        a. very
        b. most
        c. real
        d. big

6. Being able to speak conversational English proficiently is _____ guarantee you will get a high TOEFL score.

        a. no
        b. not
        c. none
        d. never

7. The TOEFL writing section _____ two tasks: the independent and the integrated writing tasks.

    a. wants to
    b. knows of
    c. belongs to
    d. consists of

8. The TOEFL writing raters _____ to rate your responses objectively.

    a. are taught
    b. are trained
    c. are available
    d. are interested

9. Beth took three TOEFL classes. _____ , she had a private tutor.

    a. For example
    b. However
    c. As a result
    d. Moreover

10. If you have a problem while taking the TOEFL test, notify the test center manager immediately by _____ your hand.

    a. raising
    b. rising
    c. putting
    d. sticking

11. Before you take the TOEFL test, contact the schools _____ you are applying and ask what their TOEFL requirements are.

    a. on which
    b. to which
    c. by which
    d. for which

12. If you are caught cheating on the TOEFL test in the United States, you will pay a $250,000.00 fine, go to jail for six months, and _____ permanently barred from entering the United States.

    a. be
    b. are
    c. will
    d. is

Written Expression → Exercise #2

<u>Task</u>: Identify the error in each passage. Check your answers on page 204.

1. <u>TOEFL is not only</u> an academic English language proficiency test, <u>but also</u> a
        A   B
   <u>time manager test</u>. That means you <u>must always watch the clock</u>.
         C   D

2. <u>There is a big difference</u> between <u>conversational English</u> and academic English.
            A   B
   One is informal <u>when</u> the <u>other</u> is formal.
                  C   D

3. Joe <u>has</u> always been a fast worker, <u>whereas</u> Mary prefers <u>to take her time</u> and
         A   B   C
   think things <u>threw</u>.
            D

4. The TOEFL <u>listening section</u> consists of three lectures, <u>one discussion</u>, and
             A   B
   two conversations, one <u>of which</u> is informal <u>while</u> the other is formal.
                     C   D

5. <u>How is your</u> English typing? On test day, you <u>will type</u> your two written res-
        A   B
   ponses using an old-style Microsoft <u>computer</u>, which is <u>not touch sensitive</u>.
                             C   D

6. TOEFL <u>tests</u> automaticity. Defined, automaticity is your <u>ability to apply</u> aca-
          A   B
   demic English <u>with out</u> pausing <u>to translate</u>.
              C   D

7. <u>Rhetorical</u> <u>strategies</u> are essential <u>for</u> <u>the</u> TOEFL success.
        A   B   C D

8. <u>An example of a</u> reading passage topic <u>might be a</u> comparison <u>between</u> the
           A   B   C
   earth, the moon, and <u>the son</u>.
                      D

9. <u>An argument it is</u> an attempt <u>to persuade an audience</u> that your position, de-
           A   B
   pending <u>upon</u> the topic, is right, good, <u>and true</u>.
          C   D

10. <u>Remember</u> that <u>the main topic</u> and <u>the main idea</u> be the <u>same thing</u>.
         A   B   C   D

11. I am disagree with that statement.
    A   B   C   D

12. Livia is the little girl who live next door.
    A   B   C   D

13. Do you prefer to use a labtop computer or a desktop computer?
    A   B   C   D

14. A good TOEFL score is the score you need not is the score you want.
   A   B   C   D

15. The TOEFL test it is designed and administered by Educational Testing Service.
            A   B   C   D

16. Tom's friends from Canada is coming to visit him in Chicago next week
     A   B   C   D

17. Antonio thinks the TOEFL is too hard and too long.
        A   B   C   D

18. There are two types of conversation in the listening section: student and pro-
              A

    fessor, and student and stuff. The latter tests informal English while the for-
                    B   C

    mer measures your ability to answer questions based on formal English.
                                      D

19. Americans and Canadians use many different spellings, for example, Ameri-
                                 A

    cans say color, theater, bank check, and traveled while Canadian use the
                                     B

    British spelling of colour, theatre, bank cheque, and travelled.
     C   D

20. The professor suspicious the student of plagiarism.
     A   B   C   D

21. After she gets her undergraduate degree, Clara is not sure if she wants to do
           A   B   C

    a master's degree or no.
       D

22. Your phone is a distractor, so remember to turn if off when you study for
             A   B

    TOEFL in order to concentrate more fully on the task at hand.
              C   D

Vocabulary → Exercise #2

Task: Choose the correct synonym. Check your answers on page 205.

1. ample (adj)

   a. some
   b. enough
   c. a few
   d. infinite

2. obstacle (n)

   a. goal
   b. barrier
   c. object
   d. aid

3. progeny (n)

   a. professionals
   b. children
   c. grandparents
   d. parents

4. famine (n)

   a. familiar food
   b. a balance of food
   c. plenty of food
   d. severe lack of food

5. conundrum (n)

   a. solution
   b. solvent
   c. problem
   d. protest

6. coalesce (v)

   a. condense
   b. confess
   c. condemn
   d. combine

7. opponent (n)

   a. member
   b. associate
   c. supporter
   d. rival

8. incessant (adj)

   a. rarely doing
   b. never stopping
   c. effortless
   d. careful planning

9. exemplary (adj)

   a. outlandish
   b. outstanding
   c. outrageous
   d. encouraging

10. prevalent (adj)

    a. fast
    b. common
    c. fun happy
    d. perfect

11. voluminous (adj)

    a. large
    b. small
    c. average
    d. tiny

12. frivolous (adj)

    a. not serious
    b. not thinking
    c. not working
    d. not buying

13. conscious of (adj)

    a. being alone in
    b. being talked to
    c. being aware of
    d. being ask to

14. morose (adj)

    a. smiling
    b. quiet
    c. happy
    d. sad

15. respite (n)

    a. relaxing pause
    b. exhausting work
    c. boring moment
    d. interesting time

16. acquire (v)

    a. to miss
    b. to lose
    c. to get
    d. to guess

17. misanthrope (n)

    a. hater of people
    b. liker of people
    c. teacher of people
    d. ruler of people

18. era (n)

    a. extra time
    b. time out
    c. time off
    d. time period

Structure → Exercise #3

<u>Task</u>: Fill in the blanks with the correct words. Check your answers on page 206.

1. Which person has been the _____ influence in your life?

    a. great
    b. grader
    c. greatest
    d. greater

2. On test day, you cannot use your own pen and paper to take notes. Note paper and pencils _____ supplied.

    a. will have been
    b. will
    c. will have had
    d. will be

3. When taking the TOEFL test, do not use an idiom if you are not 100% sure of its meaning and the context _____ it is used.

    a. of which
    b. in which
    c. on which
    d. whereas

4. Eating out has both positive and negative _____ . What are they? Why? Develop your argument using examples and reasons.

    a. expects
    b. insects
    c. aspects
    d. connects

5. Personally, I think there are advantages and disadvantages _____ a car.

    a. to be owning
    b. to owning
    c. to have owned
    d. to own

6. Do we need zoos or not? From my point of view, I believe that we need _____ .

    a. a zoo
    b. zoos
    c. the zoos
    d. the zoo

7. Telecommuting, or e-commuting, is a work _____ in which an employee works at home and is connected to his or her office by means of a telecommunications link.

> a. arrangement
> b. arranging
> c. arrange
> d. arranged

8. From my point of view, I _____ that global warming threatens all mankind.

> a. believed that
> b. believe that
> c. was believing that
> d. had been believing that

9. _____ you know that next year, six million people will die from cigarettes? That's equal to forty-seven passenger planes crashing every day for a year.

> a. Have
> b. Does
> c. Did
> d. Will

10. Thomas Edison once said, "Genius is one percent _____ and ninety-nine percent perspiration."

> a. inspired
> b. inspiration
> c. inspire
> d. insipid

11. A report in *Pediatrics* states that by age sixteen, teenagers who watch TV shows with a high degree of sexual content are twice as likely _____ babies out of wedlock than those teens who watch TV with a low degree of sexual content.

> a. to be having
> b. to be
> c. to have
> d. to get

12. Did you know that every hour three animal species _____ extinct?

> a. became
> b. will
> c. are
> d. become

Written Expression → Exercise #3

<u>Task</u>: Identify the error in each passage. Check your answers on page 206.

1. The student and <u>the professor</u> met <u>to discuss the problem</u> the student <u>had</u>
                        A   B
    <u>been have</u> with the homework, and why <u>the student had failed the last test.</u>
        C   D

2. <u>Contrary to popular belief, there are no penguins</u> <u>at the North Pole</u> just as
                      A   B   C
    <u>there is no polar bears</u> at the South Pole.
              D

3. <u>By analyzing</u> sample arguments, you will learn how the TOEFL iBT recycles
        A
    <u>opinion-based and fact-based arguments</u> for <u>testing porpoises</u> in all
                          B   C
    <u>four test sections</u>: reading, listening, speaking, and writing.
            D

4. <u>When practicing for TOEFL</u>, it is not possible to recreate test-center conditions;
                A
    <u>however, it is not possible</u> to calculate <u>a final, accurate,</u> single-number TOEFL
                      B   C
    iBT <u>score.</u>
            D

5. <u>The topics used for testing</u> are those found in first and second-year university
                        A
    life science and humanities <u>coarses,</u> <u>such as biology,</u> economics, art, geology,
                                      B   C
    zoology, literature, <u>and history.</u>
                              D

6. <u>Most U.S. and Canadian universities</u> and high schools <u>base admittance</u> on your
                        A   B
    application <u>as a hole,</u> not just on your <u>TOEFL score.</u>
                      C   D

7. <u>An argument which</u> successfully persuades demonstrates <u>coherence.</u> Coherence
              A   B
    means the argument <u>is clear and logical</u> because <u>it demonstrates proficiently.</u>
                                C   D

8. When a speaker or a writer <u>makes a conclusion</u> based on his/her opinion and
                                    A
<u>supporting illustrations</u>, he/she is using deduction <u>as the method of organizing</u>
        B   C
his/her <u>arguing</u>.
        D

9. When making tea, <u>first boil water</u>. Next, put <u>a tea bag into a cup</u>. When the
                        A   B
water is boiling, pour the water <u>into a cup</u>. Finally, add milk and sugar as
                                    C
<u>you prefer</u>.
     D

10. <u>For the TOEFL</u> speaking and writing tasks, <u>you must identify</u> and apply rea-
       A   B
sons <u>when developing</u>, delivering, <u>or summarizing arguments</u>.
        C   D

11. <u>When a speaker or a writer</u> starts <u>an argument by examples</u>—then makes a
         A   B
conclusion <u>based on those examples</u>—he/she is using induction as the method
              C
of organizing <u>his/her argument</u>.
              D

12. <u>ETS, the company who designs</u> the TOEFL iBT, <u>says that the TOEFL iBT</u> is "an
        A   B
integrated test." Integrated, <u>according to ETS</u>, means testing four skill sets
                                    C
(reading, listening, speaking, writing) <u>by combining them in various tasks</u>.
                                          D

13. <u>How would you make</u> the world <u>a bitter place</u>? <u>Give examples</u> and reasons to
        A   B   C
support <u>and</u> develop your position.
        D

<table>
<tr><td>1</td><td rowspan="9">14. Topical unity means <u>you focus at one topic</u> from start to finish. If you sud-
                           A

denly introduce a new and unrelated topic, <u>you are changing topics</u>. For exam-
                                            B

ple, <u>you are writing about pizza when you suddenly change to TOEFL</u>. This ob-
                            C

vious change in topic direction is called a topic digression. This will result in a

lack of <u>topical unity and coherence</u>.
                        D</td></tr>
<tr><td>2</td></tr>
<tr><td>3</td></tr>
<tr><td>4</td></tr>
<tr><td>5</td></tr>
<tr><td>6</td></tr>
<tr><td>7</td></tr>
<tr><td>8</td></tr>
<tr><td>9</td></tr>
</table>

<u>Vocabulary</u> → **Exercise #3**

<u>Task</u>: Choose the correct synonym. Check your answers on page 206.

1. brevity (n)

    a. concise
    b. neat
    c. tidy
    d. long

2. zeal (n)

    a. apathy
    b. laziness
    c. enthusiasm
    d. indifference

3. suppose (v)

    a. assume
    b. assail
    c. assay
    d. ask

4. eccentric (adj)

    a. lovable
    b. average
    c. strange
    d. wonderful

5. shame (n)

    a. shock
    b. joy
    c. vision
    d. dishonor

6. gauge (v)

    a. make
    b. break
    c. measure
    d. encourage

7. torpor (n)

    a. top
    b. hope
    c. boredom
    d. sleepiness

8. connote (v)

    a. dream
    b. conspire
    c. conceal
    d. suggest

9. candid (adj)

    a. shy
    b. frank
    c. brave
    d. bold

10. dearth of (adj)

    a. a lot of
    b. a lack of
    c. a need for
    d. to die for

11. denote (v)

    a. damage
    b. represent
    c. destroy
    d. reveal

12. albeit (conj)

    a. plus
    b. and
    c. moreover
    d. however

13. kindle (v)

    a. to end
    b. to incline
    c. to start
    d. to kill

14. ingenious (adj)

    a. innovative
    b. stupid
    c. weak
    d. happy

15. achieve (v)

    a. gain
    b. lose
    c. win
    d. tie

16. striking (adj)

    a. noticeable
    b. hidden
    c. ready
    d. fun

17. ancestors (n)

    a. past family
    b. present family
    c. large family
    d. royal family

18. stigmatize (v)

    a. improve
    b. mark
    c. note
    d. stick

Structure → Exercise #4

Task: Fill in the blank with the correct word. Check your answers on page 207.

1. When the preparation clock _____ zero, you will hear a "Beep!"

    a. finds
    b. touches
    c. reaches
    d. breaks

2. In the dialogue, a student _____ Environmental Club reminds her professor that he is supposed to talk to her club about his latest research.

    a. from the
    b. from a
    c. from an
    d. from

3. When you give your opinion, speak subjectively using _____ person and the present tense.

    a. third
    b. only
    c. second
    d. first

4. What if you think the suggested solutions are not good _____? What if you have a better solution?

    a. enough
    b. one
    c. example
    d. sense

5. Crude oil is black or dark brown and consists of naturally occurring hydrocarbons and _____ organic compounds.

    a. another
    b. less
    c. other
    d. very

6. With the increasing demand for oil, oil companies are now drilling offshore in areas once thought _____ dangerous for oil operations.

    a. too
    b. at
    c. often
    d. is

7. _____ the water around seamounts is nutrient-rich, a great variety of plants and fish make seamounts their home.

    a. Even though
    b. However
    c. A lot
    d. Because

8. The students discuss two solutions to the woman's problem. Describe the problem, _____ which solution you prefer and why.

    a. than state
    b. then state
    c. and state
    d. they state

9. When you summarize the problem and the solutions, _____ objectively using third person and the present tense.

    a. summarizing them
    b. summary them
    c. summarize them
    d. summarize it

10. For this task, you will listen to a lecture on an academic topic. After you listen to the lecture, you will answer a question _____ the topic in the lecture.

    a. based on
    b. found out
    c. touched on
    d. learned about

11. In 1793, Eli Whitney _____ the cotton gin and revolutionized the cotton in-dustry in the American south.

    a. invented
    b. invaded
    c. acted upon
    d. thought about

12. _____ DNA from old bones is a complicated and time-consuming process.

    a. Investing
    b. Replacing
    c. Extracting
    d. Borrowing

13. Pangea was a supercontinent that existed approximately 250 _____ years ago.

    a. millions
    b. thousands
    c. hundreds
    d. million

14. In the mid-_____ century, two influential art movements emerged: Impressionism in France and the Pre-Raphaelite Brotherhood in England.

    a. ninteenth
    b. nineteenth
    c. neinteeth
    d. nineteeht

15. Revolution 1.0 and 2.0 refer to the Tunisian and Egyptian revolutions of 2011, popular uprisings _____ social media to spread their messages.

    a. which used
    b. who used
    c. which made
    d. that could

16. Picasso moved through three stylistic _____ : Blue, Rose, and African.

    a. zones
    b. periods
    c. eras
    d. idea

17. British and German castles represent two distinct _____ of medieval architecture.

    a. stories
    b. styles
    d. beliefs
    d. colors

18. Abraham Maslow believed that humans _____ unsatisfied needs.

    a. are motivated by
    b. is motivated by
    c. motivated by
    d. can be motivited by

Written Expression → Exercise #4

<u>Task</u>: Identify the error in each passage. Check your answers on page 207.

1. <u>Carefully</u> read the prompt. <u>Make sure</u> you understand <u>them</u> before you
     A   B   C
   <u>respond</u>.
    D

2. <u>In order to</u> reduce <u>the schools carbon footprint</u>, and to reduce the spiraling
     A   B
   cost of pulp-based text books, <u>the campus bookstore</u> <u>will go digital</u> starting
                                C   D
   next semester.

3. <u>The man gives his opinion</u> about <u>new policy</u>. <u>State his position</u> and explain
          A   B   C
   the reasons he gives <u>for holding that opinion</u>.
                       D

4. <u>Animal's behavior</u> can be classified <u>according to</u> the time of day <u>an animal</u> is
       A   B   C
   <u>active</u>.
    D

5. <u>Next is micro bats</u>. As the name implies, <u>micro bats are quite small</u>, about
       A   B
   the size of a mouse. To find food, <u>micro bats use echolocation</u>, high frequency
                                 C
   sounds <u>they bounce off insects</u>.
          D

6. J. D. Salinger, <u>an</u> eccentric recluse, penned *The Catcher in the Rye*, a seminal,
             A
   <u>coming-of-age novel</u> which introduced <u>a new literature character</u>: the rebellious
        B   C
   <u>teenager</u>.
    D

7. <u>The speaker paraphrases</u> the main points in the reading <u>and demonstrates</u>
         A   B
   sentence variety, <u>for example</u>, a complex sentence <u>with an adverb clause</u> of
               C   D
   reason.

8. The term bestseller describes a book that is popular because it sells well
         A   B

    hence the term bestseller. Bestsellers can be fiction or none-fiction. The most
                                             C

    famous bestseller list in America is *The New York Times* bestseller list.
                              D

9. Refining is an industrial process whereby crude oil—raw, unprocessed oil tak-
                                        A

    en directly from the ground—is refined to usable petroleum products, such as
               B   C

    gasoline, diesel fuel, asphalt, heating oil, and liquefied naturil gas.
                                                   D

10. Before European settlers arrived in North America, the cowbird followed the
      A

    buffalo across the Great Plains, to eat the insects stirred up by the passing
                                            B

    herds. In this way, cowbirds were nomadic, always on the move in search of
                                   C

    food, much like the buffalo.
               D

11. Seamounts are undersea mountains rising on the ocean floor. Seamounts
                                                A

    range in height from 1,000 meters to over 4,000 meters. Worldwide, there are
                                        B

    approximately 100,000 seamounts, most of which have not been mapped.
      C   D

12. The American Civil War was fighted between the northern and the southern
                          A   B   C

    states from 1861 to 1865. It started when the South withdrew from the Union.
                                  D

13. The Green Revolution of the 1960's had one goal: to eliminate famine world-
                                        A

    wide. It did so by introducing the concept of industrialized agriculture. Prior to
                                                   B

    the Green Revolution, farming in less developing nations had changed little
                                      C

    since man first planted seeds.
                 D

14. The professor and the student discuss two solutions to the students problem.
                                       A   B

    Identify the problem, then state which solution you prefer and why.
      C   D

<u>Vocabulary</u> → **Exercise #4**

<u>Task</u>: Choose the correct synonym. Check your answers on page 208.

1. organize (v)

   a. to add
   b. to appear
   c. to orchestrate
   d. to empower

2. external (adj)

   a. between
   b. beside
   c. inside
   d. outside

3. predict (v)

   a. foretell
   b. believe
   c. encourage
   d. prepare

4. evaluate (v)

   a. assess
   b. choose
   c. specify
   d. descend

5. trend (n)

   a. formula
   b. plan
   c. shape
   d. direction

6. notion (n)

   a. notes
   b. idea
   c. symbol
   d. notable

7. principle (n)

   a. knowledge
   b. pinnacle
   c. educator
   d. theory

8. value (n)

   a. worth
   b. coast
   c. profit
   d. money

9. modify (v)

   a. moderate
   b. destroy
   c. change
   d. manage

10. confess (v)

   a. create
   b. contest
   c. determine
   d. admit

11. subsequently (adv)

   a. following
   b. leading
   c. knowing
   d. trying

12. justify (v)

   a. prove
   b. avoid
   c. educate
   d. act on

13. egregious (adj)

   a. shocking
   b. wonderful
   c. excellent
   d. admirable

14. region (n)

   a. system
   b. signal
   c. sector
   d. rule

15. impact (n)

   a. collision
   b. accident
   c. incident
   d. vision

16. proponent (n)

   a. co-worker
   b. supporter
   c. professional
   d. antagonist

17. potential (n)

   a. tension
   b. strength
   c. wisdom
   d. possibility

18. characteristic (adj)

   a. conclusion
   b. theory
   c. child-like
   d. feature

Structure → Exercise #5

Task: Fill in the blanks with the correct words. Check your answers on page 208.

1. The American Revolution of 1776 had one aim: to defeat the British, then _____ a government that would put the Thirteen Colonies on the path to nationhood.

       a. abolish
       b. establish
       c. relish
       d. polish

2. According to ETS, each verbal response _____ by 3 certified raters.

       a. is analyzed
       b. will be deleted
       c. is rated
       d. will be written

3. The listening section measures your ability to understand "authentic speech patterns" _____ academic (formal) and non-academic (informal) contexts.

       a. suggested in
       b. tested in
       c. taught in
       d. used in

4. The clock will not run _____ listen to a conversation or a lecture. The clock will run only when you answer questions.

       a. as you
       b. when it
       c. only while
       d. as they

5. When answering questions, do not look for perfect answers. There are no perfect answers on the TOEFL iBT. _____ , look for the closest possible answer.

       a. Also
       b. Instead
       c. Moreover
       d. In addition

6. On test day, you _____ the questions as you listen to the conversations and lectures.

       a. will not
       b. will be free to
       c. will be listening to
       d. will not see

7. As you know, cause-and-effect relationships _____ reasons.

    a. cause
    b. create
    c. define
    d. describe

8. Details are _____ information.

    a. general
    b. specific
    c. perfect
    d. external

9. To understand an idiom's function, you must infer its meaning specific to the context in which the idiom is used. This process is called _____ .

    a. analyzing
    b. calculating
    c. contextualizing
    d. prioritizing

10. Tone describes the feeling in a speaker's voice. For TOEFL, tone can include doubt, surprise, disbelief, excitement, anger, and relief. From a speaker's tone, you can infer _____ .

    a. meaning
    b. answers
    d. examples
    d. structures

11. The listening section will include four academic lectures. Each lecture will last approximately five minutes. Each lecture will be _____ six questions.

    a. designed with
    b. based on
    c. preceded by
    d. followed by

12. Inferred attitude means the speaker's opinion or position is not stated as fact in the conversation. Instead, it is _____ or implied.

    a. suggested
    b. written
    d. added
    c. highlighted

Written Expression → Exercise #5

Task: Identify the error in each passage. Check your answers on page 208.

1. Pathos is an appeal <u>to the emotions</u>. <u>By appealing to</u> the emotions, the arguer
   A   B

   can evoke sympathy <u>from an audience</u>. Sympathy, in turn, makes an argument
             C

   <u>more than</u> persuasive.
      D

2. On October 3, 1990, East <u>and</u> West <u>German</u> united <u>after</u> 45 years of <u>separation</u>.
             A   B   C   D

3. <u>Extracting</u> oil <u>from</u> olives <u>begins with</u> <u>perfect</u> ripened olives.
     A   B   C   D

4. <u>At</u> 29,029 feet, Mount Everest <u>is</u> the world's <u>highest</u> <u>montain</u>.
   A   B   C   D

5. <u>Much archeologists</u> believe that climate change <u>led to</u> the extinction of the Ne-
        A   B

   anderthals and <u>the rise of</u> Homo Sapiens, <u>particularly in</u> Europe.
          C   D

6. Today, <u>the Sahara Dessert</u> is a sun-baked sea of sand, <u>whereas in 7,000 BC</u>,
         A   B

   the Sahara <u>was a fertile zone</u> covered with lakes and <u>savannah</u>.
          C   D

7. <u>Simply put</u>, the human genome is <u>an organism</u> hereditary database <u>encoded</u>
      A   B   C

   in the organism's <u>DNA and RNA</u>.
            D

8. Pervasive development disorders <u>includes</u> autism, Asperger syndrome, Rett
             A

   syndrome, <u>childhood</u> disintegrative disorder (CDD), and <u>persuasive</u> develop-
        B   C

   mental <u>disorder</u>.
       D

9. Ordering questions <u>are detail questions</u>. They measure your ability to identify
          A

   the steps <u>in a process or event</u>, such as a moment <u>in history</u> or the stages in a
         B   C

   person's or an <u>animal's lives</u>.
        D

10. The professor <u>describes</u> how plastic becomes part <u>in the eco-system</u>. Put those
              A   B
<u>steps in order</u>. This is <u>a 2-point question</u>.
   C   D

11. Every year, Americans <u>buy over</u> 50 billion—yes, billion—<u>bottles of water</u>. That
                           A   B
<u>equates</u> to 1,500 bottles <u>consuming</u> every second.
  C   D

12. <u>In the lecture</u>, what is mentioned <u>about penguins</u>? Select <u>tree</u>. This is a 2-
   A   B   C
point <u>question</u>.
     D

Notes

Vocabulary → Exercise #5

Task: Choose the correct synonym. Check your answers on page 209.

1. evolve (v)

   a. develop
   b. determine
   c. detract
   d. distract

2. congeal (v)

   a. solidify
   b. melt
   c. break
   d. shatter

3. buckle down (v)

   a. get mad
   b. go away
   c. take charge
   d. get serious

4. arbitrary (adj)

   a. argument
   b. for a reason
   c. accidental
   d. without reason

5. recede (v)

   a. remember
   b. refresh
   c. reform
   d. retreat

6. veracity (n)

   a. truthfulness
   b. earnestness
   c. fearlessness
   d. happiness

7. accurately (adv)

   a. poorly
   b. precisely
   c. progressively
   d. painfully

8. deify (v)

   a. worship
   b. impress
   c. verify
   d. desire

9. let go of (v)

   a. release
   b. decrease
   c. control
   d. wordy

10. implement (v)

    a. perform
    b. prevent
    c. put off
    d. pan

11. build up (v)

    a. renovate
    b. attack
    c. decrease
    d. increase

12. chronic (adj)

    a. periodically
    b. rarely
    c. constantly
    d. intermittently

13. remote (adj)

    a. isolated
    b. familiar
    c. popular
    d. nearby

14. refute (v)

    a. to support
    b. to argue against
    c. to argue precisely
    d. to avoid arguing

15. lethal (adj)

    a. friendly
    b. deadly
    c. legally
    d. injection

16. assumption (n)

    a. conclusion
    b. concussion
    c. contrition
    d. contrarian

17. pestilence (n)

    a. contagion
    b. bean
    c. newspaper
    d. beverage

18. conjecture (n)

    a. understand
    b. vision
    c. conclusion
    d. speculation

Structure → Exercise #6

Task: Fill in the blanks with the correct answers. Check your answers on page 209.

1. When you skim a paragraph, you _____ general information. That information is in the topic sentence. Read the topic sentence, then jump (skim) over the example and read the conclusion. _____ conclusion will restate the topic introduced _____ topic sentence.

   1. a. read for
      b. read at
      c. read into
      d. read a

   2. a. Maybe the
      b. Never will the
      c. Rarely will the
      d. Often the

   3. a. in an
      b. in the
      c. in a
      d. in about the

2. You now have two choices left. This is the position TOEFL wants you _____ . You now have a good chance _____ the correct answer. But which one is it? Both sound good. However, one is correct _____ is the distractor.

   1. a. to be not
      b. to be at
      c. to be on
      d. to be in

   2. a. of making
      b. of choosing
      c. of mistaking
      d. of avoiding

   3. a. and the next
      b. and another
      c. and the other
      d. or the other

3. In 1928, _____ scientist Alexander Fleming _____ *Penicillium notatum* contained a bacteria-killing antibiotic, an antibiotic Fleming _____ penicillin.

   1. a. Scotland
      b. Scottish
      c. Scott's
      d. Scotish

   2. a. discovered that
      b. taught that
      c. knew that
      d. forgot that

   3. a. created
      b. named
      c. said
      d. the

4. In 1929, Fleming published the _____ his experiments in the British Journal of Experimental Pathology. _____ such initial promise, his work attracted little attention, for growing penicillium was difficult while extracting the antibiotic agent, the bacteria-killing penicillin itself, was _____ .

   1. a. story of
      b. results of
      c. mystery of
      d. problems of

   2. a. Yet despite
      b. Yet although
      c. Yet now
      d. Yet because

   3. a. even worse
      b. even though
      c. ever better
      d. even harder

5. All _____ organisms _____ Earth, including humans, are carbon and water-based cellular _____ .

   1. a. alive
      b. living
      c. to be alive
      d. lived

   2. a. in
      b. on
      c. upon
      d. onto

   3. a. structures
      b. shapes
      c. things
      d. organs

6. Objects that do not signal a self-sustaining biological process _____ inanimate, such as rocks, or dead. For an organism to be a self-sustaining biological process, it _____ a metabolism, a metabolism being a series of integrated chemical processes, _____ enable the organism to maintain an input-output balance called homeostasis.

1. a. are neither	2. a. should be	3. a. which
b. are always	b. might have	b. who can
c. are both	c. must have	c. that
d. are either	d. will have	d. wherein

7. In 1735, Carl Linnaeus, a Swedish botanist and zoologist _____ establishing binomial nomenclature (the naming of species), believed there were two kingdoms: Vegetabilia and Animalia. Today that list _____ to six: Bacteria (prokaryotes), Protozoa (eukaryotes), Chromista (a eukaryotic supergroup), Fungi (eukaryotic organisms, _____ yeasts molds and mushrooms), Plantae (such as trees, herbs, bushes, grasses), and Animalia (multicellular eukaryotic organisms).

1. a. worked at	2. a. have grown	3. a. indeed
b. determined to	b. will have grown	b. another
c. infamous for	c. has grown	c. such as
d. credited with	d. was grown	d. plus

8. Primates are mammals that have large brains, _____ two or four limbs and rely on stereoscopic vision. In Order Primates, _____ two distinct classifications called Families: Hominidae (hominids) and Cercopithecidae. Cercopithecidae are Old World monkeys native to Asia and Africa, monkeys such as baboons and macaques while Family Hominidae _____ the great apes (gorillas, chimpanzees, orangutans) and humans.

1. a. walk on	2. a. there are	3. a. represents
b. walk with	b. there is	b. symbolizes
c. walk around	c. there will be	c. synthesizes
d. walk onto	d. there was	d. socializes

9. For TOEFL, if you have "a feeling" you know the right answer, _____ feeling. Your "feeling" is your passive English vocabulary talking to you. Classroom experience proves that test-takers often trust their feelings, but then go back and _____ answers only to realize that they had made the right choice all along. This strategy applies _____ TOEFL tasks.

1. a. live for your	2. a. change their	3. a. to all the
b. trust your	b. confuse their	b. to all those
c. feel for your	c. think about their	c. to only
d. talk about your	d. delete their	d. to all

10. _____ infer the meaning of a word by its sound. For example, night _____ sound exactly the same but have completely _____ meanings.

1. a. You must
   b. Do not
   c. Of course you
   d. Please

2. a. or knight
   b. and a knight
   c. and knight
   d. and the knight

3. a. difficult
   b. difference
   c. different
   d. different from

11. You can infer the meaning of a word, phrase, or idiom by identifying synonyms _____ . A synonym in context means that a word and its synonym will be used within the same context. For example, read the highlighted sentence in sample paragraph. Note the highlighted word *gauge*. _____ measure. Note that a synonym of *gauge* is Measuring. This is _____ a synonym in context.

1. a. in context
   b. in stuff
   c. in conflict
   d. in position

2. a. Gauge is
   b. Gauge means
   c. Gauge can be
   d. Gauge explains

3. a. an example
   b. an example that
   c. an example of
   d. an example from

12. _____ , flooding has caused untold human misery and destruction. Witness the Central China floods of 1931, the greatest natural disaster _____ . Three rivers flooded and left over three million people dead. Yet without flooding, we _____ be where we are today.

1. a. Forever
   b. For centuries
   c. For a while
   d. For a time

2. a. ever
   b. ever survived
   c. ever seen
   d. ever recorded

3. a. ought to
   b. will
   c. should
   d. would not

Notes

_____

_____

_____

_____

_____

_____

_____

_____

_____

_____

_____

<u>Written Expression</u> → Exercise #6

<u>Task</u>: Identify the error in each passage. Check your answers on page 209.

1   1.   Everyone <u>knows that America</u> put the first man on the moon. What most don't
2   A
3   realize, however, is that the Saturn V, the launch rocket <u>that sent Apollo 11</u>
4   B
5   astronauts Neil Armstrong, Buzz Aldrin and Michael Collins to the moon, <u>was</u>
6
7   <u>designed by Germans</u>, in particular <u>the space architecture</u> and Nazi rocket sci-
8   C   D
9   entist Wernher Von Braun.

2.   <u>The process of</u> checking and verifying four answer choices <u>is time consuming</u>.
         A   B
       Watch the clock. <u>If the question</u> is giving you trouble, or taking too much
                           C
       time, guess and move on. <u>You will not be penaltied</u> for a wrong answer.
                                      D

3.   <u>Analysis the question</u> and each answer choice carefully. Classroom experience
          A
       proves that many test-takers <u>select the wrong answer</u> <u>because</u> they did not
                                     B   C
       take the time <u>to check and verify</u> each answer choice.
                        D

1   4.   Jane Austen's novel *Pride and Prejudice*, voted Best British novel in a 2005
2
3   BBC poll, <u>was originally titled *First Impressions*</u>. Austen wrote it between Octo-
4   A
5   ber 1796 and <u>August 1797</u>. The story centers on the Bennett family, particu-
6   B
7   larly the five sisters <u>who's mother, Mrs. Bennett</u>—a mercurial soul always on
8   C
9   the verge of nervous collapse—is determined to marry them off to rich hus-
10
11   bands thus ensuring their financial futures while securing for them positions
12
13   <u>of high social status in early nineteenth century England</u>.
                            D

5. These days it is common to see biologists on TV studying animals in the wild up close, so close it is as if the human observer <u>was part of</u> the animal
   A
   group <u>being studied</u>. One of the scientists <u>to first bridge the gap</u> between <u>wild</u>
   B   C   <u>animals and a human observer</u> was Dian Fossey.
   D

6. There are two methods of research: <u>qualitative and quantitative</u>. Qualitative
   A
   research <u>is based on events</u> observed by the researcher <u>while</u> quantitative re-
   B   C
   searched <u>is based on numerous data</u> gathered by the researcher.
   D

7. <u>To produce reliable and credible research</u>, a researcher using the qualitative
   A
   approach focuses on <u>the why and how of decision making</u>, specifically in re-
   B
   gard to human behavior, such as why a child will sit in front of a computer for
   hours at a time <u>or how a tribe of Amazonian Indians</u> deals with a threat to its
   C
   territory <u>from a neighborhood tribe</u>.
   D

8. Crypsis, <u>the ability of an organism to avoid being seen</u> by another organism,
   A
   can be achieved through camouflage and mimicry. Camouflage means hiding
   <u>by blending in with the environment</u>. An organism that employs camouflage is
   B
   <u>the tawny frogmouth of Australian</u>. When seen, the tawny frogmouth is often
   C
   confused with an owl; <u>however, it is not an owl but a nightjar</u>.
   D

9. In January, 2010, <u>the Supreme Court of the United States</u> ruled on the case
   A
   the US Supreme Court vs. the Federal Elections Commission. In this landmark
   ruling, the bitterly-divided Court ruled 5-4 <u>that corporations enjoy</u> the same
   B
   First Amendment rights <u>as will individuals</u>. In other words, a corporation,
   C
   no matter what the size, <u>is considered a citizen</u>.
   D

10. In 2004, <u>Oscar-winning documentary film</u> Michael Moore <u>released</u> *Fahrenheit*
                 A   B

    911, a scathing attacked <u>on how</u> Republican President George W. Bush failed
                           C

    <u>to act during the 9/11 crisis.</u>
                D

11. <u>Each reading passage</u> will have <u>2 or fewer rhetorical-purpose questions</u>. These
            A   B

    questions measure your ability <u>to identification how</u> the writer uses rhetorical
                                 C

    strategies <u>to develop an argument.</u>
              D

12. <u>Passing judgment is human nature.</u> Some of our judgments are accurate while
                A

    others are flawed because we did not take the time <u>to think the issue through</u>
                                 B

    and instead <u>make the snap decision</u> based on experience. A snap decision re-
              C

    sulting in an error of judgment <u>is called a cognitive bias.</u>
                                D

Notes

_____

_____

_____

_____

_____

_____

_____

_____

_____

_____

_____

_____

_____

_____

_____

Vocabulary → Exercise #6

Task: Choose the correct synonym. Check your answers on page 210.

1. affluent (adj)

    a. poor
    b. average
    c. wealthy
    d. respected

2. elevate (v)

    a. raise
    b. balance
    c. level
    d. remove

3. amiable (adj)

    a. friendly
    b. mean
    c. indifferent
    d. tidy

4. annex (v)

    a. separate
    b. join
    c. reveal
    d. demonstrate

5. drought (n)

    a. wet period
    b. dry period
    c. cold period
    d. old period

6. welfare (n)

    a. state of being
    b. state of knowing
    c. state of learning
    d. state of seeing

7. decay (v)

    a. break down
    b. break out
    c. break off
    d. break into

8. quaint (adj)

    a. old style
    b. new style
    c. no style
    d. stylish

9. avarice (n)

    a. greed
    b. need
    c. seed
    d. feed

10. plagiarize (v)

    a. to copy directly
    b. to buy illegally
    c. to sell indirectly
    d. to take illegally

11. abdicate (v)

    a. give off
    b. give out
    c. give up
    d. give away

12. concoct (v)

    a. invent
    b. bend
    c. cause
    d. conform

13. crude (adj)

    a. fragile
    b. brittle
    c. smooth
    d. rough

14. concept (n)

    a. challenge
    b. problem
    c. idea
    d. reward

15. acquiesce (v)

    a. questions always
    b. fight violently
    c. submit quietly
    d. ask often

16. deity (n)

    a. heaven
    b. god
    c. diet
    d. deed

17. enmity (n)

    a. preference
    b. hatred
    c. desire
    d. suspicion

18. prevalent (adj)

    a. typical
    b. normal
    c. strange
    d. common

Structure → Exercise #7

Task: Fill in the blanks with the correct answers. Check your answers on page 210.

1. The verb *to gild* means to apply a layer of gold to an object. Mark Twain used _____ form of this verb when he coined the phrase the Gilded Age. The Gilded Age, _____ , represents American economic prosperity at its height. And for good reason. The Gilded Age created many firsts, such as a new class of super-rich, _____ John D. Rockefeller.

1. a. the adjective	2. a. from 1869 or 1893	3. a. men more like
b. the adverbial	b. from 1869 and 1893	b. men who are
c. the adjectival	c. from 1869 to the 1893	c. men only like
d. the phrasal	d. from 1869 to 1893	d. men like

2. One consumer item that changed millions of women's lives was the Singer sewing machine. By 1880, over three million _____ Singer. Why was this invention so revolutionary? Prior to the Singer sewing machine, women _____ and make clothes for their families, a time-consuming task that left women with little free time for anything else. Yet the Singer sewing machine changed all that. It not only sped up the clothes-making process, but also led to the development of textile factories where clothes, such as those for railroad workers, were mass produced. _____ that clothes were machine-made and women, no longer having to make clothes, had more time for politics.

1. a. offices had an	2. a. had to stay home	3. a. The result is
b. places have a	b. had to buy a home	b. The result was
c. homes had a	c. had to rent a home	c. The results were
d. companies had a	d. had to get married	d. This resulted in

3. _____ disagree that violent video games are designed with killing in mind, just like no one would disagree that problem-solution scenarios, _____ an anti-hero shoots and kills his way to freedom, _____ detrimental behavior in adolescents.

1. a. Nobody should	2. a. in which	3. a. reinforced
b. Somebody shall	b. of which	b. reinforces
c. Nobody would	c. by which	c. reinforcement
d. Anybody might	d. which is	d. reinforce

4. _____ days, doctors are _____ antibiotics for the common cold. Instead, doctors _____ the body heal itself.

1. a. When	2. a. prescribing less	3. a. prefer that
b. Those	b. prescribing much	b. believe that
c. would	c. prescribing fewer	c. know that
d. These	d. prescribing great	d. need that

5. The book *The Wealth of Nations* is very much a reaction to the predominating economic theory of the day, _____ Mercantilism. Mercantilists _____ wealth of a nation depended on developing and maintaining national power thus it was a form of economic nationalism. Spain, at the time of Columbus, is a prime example of just _____ .

1. a. that of	2. a. agreed that the	3. a. such a nation
b. which of	b. suggested that the	b. such a place
c. cause of	c. believed that the	c. such a problem
d. reason for	d. showed that the	d. such an issue

6. The comparative *fewer* is rapidly disappearing from the English language, replaced by the ubiquitous—and grammatically incorrect—*less*. For example, these days _____ to see ads that read, "Enjoy Ice Cream. It has less calories." Politicians also commit this grammatical mistake. Not a day goes by in which a politician is not screaming, "Americans need to pay less taxes!" As you know, fewer takes a _____ , such as, "Joe has *fewer problems* than Al," or "The effect of colony collapse disorder has resulted in *fewer honey bees*." Note that we can count calories (one calorie, two calories) and problems (one problem, two problems), and honey bees (one bee, two bees). *Less*, in contrast, takes a noncountable noun, such as "English teachers make far *less money* than corporate lawyers." Can we count money (one money, two monies?) No. Sadly, the word fewer will soon _____ , just like the dinosaurs.

1. a. its quite common	2. a. plural countible noun	3. a. be endangered
b. it's quiet common	b. plural countable noun	b. be saved
c. its quit common	c. plural counted noun	c. be extinct
d. it's quite common	d. plural counting noun	d. be extinguished

7. _____ park system _____ the benefit of all Americans. The parks are _____ to enjoy.

1. a. The America	2. a. was created for	3. a. theres
b. The popular	b. was tested for	b. their's
c. The American	c. was sold for	c. theirs
d. The good	d. was issued for	d. his and hers

8. _____ have determined that _____ liquid water do not exist on Mars thus there is very little water vapor _____ atmosphere.

1. a. Teachers	2. a. large bodies of	3. a. in the Martin
b. Scientists	b. large objects are	b. in the Mars
c. Priests	c. large kinds might	c. in the Martian
d. Protestors	d. large forms will	d. in the Marshian

9. Census taking is nothing new. _____ civilizations regularly took a census of population, for example Rome. Because Rome had a large army, it needed money and men. By periodically taking a census, the Roman government knew how much tax money _____ for the army and the available manpower it could draw from. It wasn't until the second half of the nineteenth century that the process of census taking

6   changed. Instead of just counting heads and money, demographers started to
7   broaden the statistic gathering to include age, occupation, marital status, _____ .

1. a. Many original	2. a. it could raise	3. a. and job
b. Many defeated	b. it could collect	b. and name
c. Many modern	c. it could neglect	c. and family
d. Many ancient	d. it could record	d. and reasons

10. Semiotics, _____ signs and symbols, _____ into the study of semantics, syntactics, _____ .

1. a. the test of	2. a. can be divided	3. a. or pragmatics
b. the mother of	b. might be divided	b. and pragmatics
c. the study of	c. should be divided	c. then pragmatics
d. the type of	d. will be divided	d. also pragmatics

11. The cowbird was originally a nomad, travelling with the buffalo and eating whatever the buffalo kicked up: insects, seeds, etc. In this light, the cowbird was very much an opportunist. _____ had a problem. Because cowbirds were nomadic, raising a family was a problem. If they stopped to raise a brood, _____ their food source, for the buffalo _____ on the move.

1. a. But the cowbird	2. a. they would lose	3. a. was always
b. But a cowbird's	b. they would loose	b. were always
c. But most cowbirds	c. they would be losing	c. were only
d. But that cowbird	d. they would have lost	d. was always

1   12. For plants to survive, _____ convert carbon dioxide into sugar using energy from
2   the sun. This conversion process is called photosynthesis. Organisms that depend
3   on photosynthesis for survival are called photoautotrophs. Plants, as well as algae
4   and many species of bacteria, _____ classification. These organisms are unique in
5   that they are the only ones to produce their own food by photosynthesis, a chemi-
6   cally complex process in which oxygen is a waste byproduct. Suffice it to say, with-
7   out photosynthesis, life on Earth would _____ .

1. a. they will	2. a. rest under this	3. a. cease to exist
b. they must	b. be under this	b. be endangered
c. they might	c. run under this	c. be interesting
d. they like to	d. fall under this	d. be disappearing

Written Expression → Exercise #7

Task: Identify the 2 errors in each passage. Check your answers on page 211.

1. Because <u>the reading passiges</u> are excerpts from actual books, there might not
    A

    be a proper introduction. The passage might instead be a series of body para-

    graphs copy-and-pasted <u>from a chapter in the book</u>. In that case, the structure
    B

    of the reading passage will be all body paragraphs. <u>No matter what the struc-</u>
    C

    <u>ture</u>, the first sentence of the first paragraph <u>will always introduce</u> the main
    D

    topic.

2. In *The Wealth of Nations*, Smith <u>argues that building national economic wealth</u>
    A

    begins with a division of labor. <u>Smith he supports his argument by using a pin</u>
    B

    <u>factory</u>. In a typical pin factory of the day, each worker was responsible for

    making pins from start to finish. A worker would start by cutting the pin to

    size from a piece of wire, <u>then straighten it, than sharpen the end</u>, affix a head,
    C

    polish it, <u>then package them</u>. In short, one man was responsible for each step
    D

    of the pin-making process.

3. <u>The rhetorical strategy of thesis-anti-thesis is recycled through</u> the TOEFL
    A

    iBT. TOEFL does so because thesis-anti-thesis is a common way to compare

    and contrast <u>two opposing arguments</u>. <u>Understanding the similarily and</u>
    B   C

    <u>differences</u> between two opposing arguments is a predictable way the TOEFL

    iBT <u>will test your ability to identify</u> how arguments are organized.
    D

4. <u>Many test-takers fell</u> that the reading section should be longer. One hour, they
    A

    say, is not enough. <u>Worst, they feel they are not reading but speed reading.</u>
    B

    <u>And they are right.</u> This is one way <u>the reading section tests you</u>. It forces you
    C   D

    to read like a native speaker under a time pressure.

9
10
11
12
13
14
15
16
17

5. To prepare for TOEFL, read English material, <u>such as newspapers, magazines,</u>
                                                                    A
<u>novels, short story, and essays</u>. Also, read for long periods of time. Reading

short, internet passages <u>is not enough for TOEFL</u>. <u>You must train</u> yourself
                          B   C
to read academic English for sustained periods of time, one or two hours at

least. <u>That way you will been test ready</u>.
         D

1
2
3

6. <u>Everybody</u> reads <u>different</u>. <u>Only by practiceing</u> will you learn <u>which reading</u>
   A   B   C   D
<u>strategy</u> is best for you.

1
2
3
4
5
6
7
8
9
10
11
12
13

7. The Socratic method, named after <u>the Greek philosophy Socrates</u>, is a meth-
                                     A
od of debate in which critical thinking is developed by asking and answering

questions in order to establish and clarify opposing viewpoints. The Socratic

method is, <u>essential</u>, a process that eliminates negative hypotheses by identify-
           B
ing contradictions in logic. This, in turn, helps <u>to shape opinions</u> and to identi-
                                                   C
fy general truths. Indeed, the Socratic method is an integral part of the western

<u>educational system</u>.
           D

1
2
3
4
5
6
7
8
9
10
11
12
13
14
15

8. In AD 476, the Western Roman Empire, its territories controlled by <u>corruption</u>
                                                                        A
<u>and ineffective governors</u>, fell to an invading army of Goths. This event was a

turning point in world history, for it marks the end of classical antiquity and

<u>the beginning of the Early Middle Ages in Europe</u>. The Early Middle Ages (circa
                          B
500 to 1,000 AD) was a time of social and economic chaos. With the collapse of

the Western Roman Empire, long distance trade was abandoned, for the trade

routes built by Rome, and <u>secured by its once-powerful army</u>, were now under
                          C
the control of varying Germanic tribes constantly <u>at war with each another</u>.
                                                    D

9. Omar Khayyám, <u>born in Persia in 1,048 AD</u>, was a polymath, a man whose
                     A
   genius ranged from astronomy to philosophy to poetry. Recognized as one of

   <u>the greatest medieval mathematicians</u>, Khayyám authored the *Treatise on Demon-*
           B
   stration of Problems of Algebra. In it, Khayyám provides a geometric method for

   solving cubic equations. Khayyám's contributions to algebra eventually found

   <u>its way to Europe</u>, as did the work of many other influential Persian mathema-
          C
   ticians <u>and schoolars</u>.
           D

10. The electric eel is an apex predator <u>found at the Amazon and Orinoco</u> Rivers of
            A
    South America. Like its name says, it is indeed electric, dangerously so. The

    charge it produces <u>can reach on to one amp at 800</u> volts, enough to incapaci-
           B
    tate <u>half a dozen people</u>. Such a lethal evolutionary attribute is produced in
        C
    body-length organs filled <u>with cells called electroplaques</u>.
            D

11. A comet—<u>a lose mixture of dust, ice, and rock particles</u>—is distinct from a me-
           A
    teorite in that a comet is a small solar system body (<u>neither a dwarf star or a</u>
           B
    <u>planet</u>), whereas a meteorite is <u>a piece of space debris that survives</u> an impact
           C
    <u>by Earth</u>.
       D

12. Each passage <u>it will have</u> one prose-summary question. This question type
           A
    measures your ability <u>to understand the passage</u> as a <u>whole</u> and complete a
           B   C
    summary <u>of that</u>. The summary will be a general outline of the passages main
           D
    ideas.

<u>Vocabulary</u> → Exercise #7

<u>Task</u>: Choose the correct synonym. Check your answers on page 211.

1. abate (v)

    a. lessen
    b. increase
    c. multiply
    d. observe

2. amalgamate (v)

    a. reject
    b. pursue
    c. combine
    d. propose

3. apprise (v)

    a. inform
    b. indicate
    c. indulge
    d. involve

4. gainsay (v)

    a. contact
    b. confuse
    c. contradict
    d. contemplate

5. commiserate with (v)

    a. fear for
    b. concern for
    c. love for
    d. sympathy for

6. neophyte (n)

    a. negotiator
    b. nightmare
    c. novice
    d. courage

7. laud (v)

    a. profit
    b. praise
    c. protect
    d. propel

8. impair (v)

    a. make worse
    b. make better
    c. make over
    d. make off

9. approbation (n)

    a. suspicion
    b. approval
    c. envy
    d. rejection

10. diverge (v)

    a. move apart
    b. move together
    c. move alone
    d. move around

11. meticulous (adj)

    a. detailed
    b. different
    c. difficult
    d. defiant

12. erudite (adj)

    a. trendy
    b. ignorant
    c. scholarly
    d. reckless

13. gullible (adj)

    a. naive
    b. wise
    c. gracious
    d. fearful

14. anarchy (n)

    a. order
    b. lawlessness
    c. freedom
    d. ancestor

15. diatribe (n)

    a. hateful look
    b. friendly greeting
    c. sweet story
    d. angry speech

16. alacrity (n)

    a. eagerness
    b. spiritless
    c. graceless
    d. fitness

17. mundane (adj)

    a. careful
    b. common
    c. comfortable
    d. crazy

18. exacerbate (v)

    a. make fun of
    b. make great
    c. make worse
    d. make excited

Structure → Exercise #8

<u>Task</u>: Fill in the blanks with the correct answers. Check your answers on page 212.

1. Logic appeals to reason. One way to appeal to reason _____ deduction. Deduction is a form of reasoning in which you make a conclusion based on a series of related facts called premises. Let's work through an example. First, you start with a major premise, such as *All English teachers are poor*. This general statement _____ a specific statement or minor premise, in this case, *Bob is an English teacher*. From these two premises, a conclusion logically follows. *Bob is poor*. Put it all together _____ reads like this: *All English teachers are poor. Bob is an English teacher. Bob _____* . As you can see, deduction can be pretty persuasive. Its closed, or formal structure, leaves no doubt as to Bob's financial situation relative to his profession.

1. a. is by using	2. a. is joined by	3. a. and	4. a. is poor
b. is by choosing	b. is fixed by	b. and it	b. was poor
c. is by lassoing	c. is taught by	c. and they	c. is richer
d. is by schmoozing	d. is followed by	d. and it's	d. is not poor

2. Samuel Dashiell Hammett _____ 1894 on a farm in Maryland. At fourteen, guided by "a rebellious temperament," he _____ school and went to work for the railroad. In 1915, at the age of twenty-one, he joined the Pinkerton Detective Agency. As a Pinkerton operative, or "Op," Hammett saw everything from "petty theft to murder." In 1918, Hammett left Pinkerton's, joined the army and _____ influenza. Soon after he developed tuberculosis. He left the army and went back to Pinkerton's but poor health forced him to resign. In 1922, weakened by disease and in need of work, Hammett, encouraged by a friend, _____ writing.

1. a. was born on	2. a. dropped by	3. a. took	4. a. turned to
b. was born in	b. dropped out of	b. have had	b. turned into
c. was born at	c. drop in on	c. started	c. turned up
d. was born when	d. dropped off	d. contracted	d. turned off

3. We Americans _____ all business cultures are like ours. Nothing could be further from the truth. Many Middle Eastern and Asian cultures prefer to do business face-to-face. Discussing business over tea or while having dinner is an integral part of the business process in these cultures. Such traditions help develop mutual respect and trust _____ between business partners but also between international employees working for the same company. Unfortunately, _____ rush for convenience and cost saving, Americans fail to appreciate that not all business cultures _____ teleconferencing as the ultimate business solution.

1. a. assimilate a	2. a. always	3. a. in the	4. a. look up
b. accept this	b. not only	b. on the	b. had
c. assign it	c. either	c. at the	c. conclusion
d. assume that	d. and	d. of the	d. view

1 4. Proponents of standardized testing are quick to wave the flag _____ statistics
2   as being the best way to measure academic performance. Yet what supporters
3   of standardized testing fail to realize is that, in their rush for statistics, they
4   have boiled education down to a game, a game _____ there are winners and
5   losers. I'm sorry, but education is not about dividing students into winners
6   and losers. It's about uniting with a focus _____ , the very thing standardized
7   testing destroys by pointing the finger at those schools _____ lower-than-
8   average scores.

1. a. of comparing	2. a. in which	3. a. on equality	4. a. when
b. of compare	b. at which	b. on students	b. with
c. of comparison	c. on which	c. on evils	c. of
d. of comparative	d. at which	d. on testing	d. about

1 5. Cell phones do not cause cancer. Period. Why not? Because cell phone radia-
2   tion _____-ionizing. What does that mean? It means that cell phone radiation
3   has too few electrons _____ cause cancer unlike ionizing radiation produced
4   by X-rays. Moreover, cell phone RF levels are tested and retested by the manu-
5   facturers to ensure that radiation levels meet the strict standards _____ Fed-
6   eral Communications Commission. That said, put to rest any _____ that you
7   might be harming yourself whenever you make a call.

1. a. is un-	2. a. that is	3. a. set by the	4. a. notion
b. is non-	b. thus cannot	b. made by a	b. hopeless
c. is re-	c. moreover it	c. owned by a	c. argue
d. is im-	d. also will	d. called by the	d. know

6. Directions: Read the following dialogue, then fill in the blanks.

1 Man: Hi, Wendy.
2 Woman: Hey, Tom. Have you heard about the new organic food policy?
3 Man: Yeah. What a great idea. It's about time the school did something to
4   improve the food around here.
5 Woman: If you ask me, I think the new policy is all wrong.
6 Man: Why?
7 Woman: Because organic food is way more expensive. In some cases, at least
8   fifty percent more. Add that to labor costs, you know, money to pay the
9   cafeteria staff, and I'm going to be paying a lot more for my coffee and the
10   milk I put in it. I hate to think _____ salad will cost. Organic may be
11   cheaper in the future, but right now it's for people with money not poor
12   students like me.
13 Man: But think of all the health benefits. You'll be eating food that doesn't
14   have any chemicals or antibiotics in it. Not only that but all that good or-
15   ganic food will be lower in fat and calories. I mean, that's got to be good,
16   right?
17 Woman: Don't be fooled. A hamburger is a hamburger whether the meat is organ-
18   ic or not. Both will have the same amount of fat and calories. The only
19   difference is the organic hamburger _____ pesticides and antibiotics.
20 Man: Well, I still think it's a good idea. By offering organic food, we'll be eating

21   a lot better. Even the snacks in the vending machines will be organic. It's
22   definitely the wave of the future. Best of all, _____ helping local farm-
23   ers.
24   <u>Woman</u>:   What I don't like is the university telling us what we can and can't eat.
25   Not everybody wants to eat organic, you know. If I want to eat non-
26   organic, that's my choice. Sorry, but the school should _____ health-
27   care business.

1. a. when a	2. a. has no	3. a. she'll be	4. a. not be in the
b. why a	b. has	b. he'll be	b. not be a
c. what a	c. has fewer	c. we'll be	c. not be the
d. whatever a	d. has less	d. they'll be	d. not be without a

1   7.   As a woman reaches middle age, _____ age 45, the estrogen level decreases.
2   Indications of decreased estrogen are hot flashes, mood swings, and weak or
3   broken bones due to a loss of bone mass. It wasn't until the early 1960's that
4   author Robert Wilson in his book *Feminine Forever* recommended that women
5   could stop the aging process _____ estrogen pills. Suddenly, women started
6   taking estrogen and were feeling much better for it. However, in the early
7   1970's, a rise in uterine cancer was connected to an increase in estrogen us-
8   age, so women stopped taking estrogen. In the late 1970's, doctors did an
9   about face and said that it was okay to take estrogen combined with another
10   hormone, progestin. By the 1990's, doctors were so enthusiastic _____ estro-
11   gen-progestin combination that they were telling women that hormone re-
12   placement therapy (HRT for short) was the solution to stopping heart attacks.
13   In short, HRT was a life-saver. By 2000, almost six million women in the Unit-
14   ed States were taking some form of HRT. That, then, is _____ history of es-
15   trogen use in America.

1. a. around	2. a. by take	3. a. about a	4. a. a brief
b. in	b. have taken	b. about the	b. a good
c. at	c. by taking	c. about in	c. a sad
d. on	d. by asking for	d. about	d. a complete

1   8.   Like most great military generals, Robert E. Lee was a gambler. Two battles
2   illustrate _____ . The first is the battle of Chancellorsville in May, 1863.
3   There, Lee broke all the rules of military engagement. Faced by a Union army
4   twice the size of his own, Lee _____ much smaller army not once, not twice,
5   but three times. In the process, Lee defeated the Union army and established
6   his reputation _____ general _____ Napoleon.

1. a. this man	2. a. repeated his	3. a. as a	4. a. equality
b. this tendency	b. developed his	b. as in	b. equal to
c. this mistake	c. added his	c. as always	c. equation
d. this thing	d. divided his	d. as much as	d. equal

1   9.   A barrel of crude oil _____ oil industry's standard unit of measurement. One
2   barrel contains 42 gallons or 159 liters. Within that barrel of crude is a com-
3   plex mixture of _____ called hydrocarbons. Hydrocarbons are what's left of
4   plants and animals that lived billions of years ago. This organic matter, deep
5   within the Earth, is heated by the Earth, which, over time, _____ crude oil
6   hence the term fossil fuel. To make consumer petroleum products from a bar-
7   rel of crude oil, products such as gasoline and diesel fuel, the hydrocarbons
8   must be separated. That separation process _____ refinery through a process
9   called fractional distillation.

1. a. is the	2. a. monocles	3. a. turns it off	4. a. is done in the
b. are the	b. mollequles	b. turns it out	b. is done at a
c. were the	c. molecules	c. turns it onto	c. is done by
d. was the	d. molesscules	d. turns it into	d. is done of a

10. Directions: Read the following dialogue, then fill in the blanks.

1   Man: Hi, Betty. What's up?
2   Woman: I got _____ Harvard law.
3   Man: Congratulations! That's fantastic.
4   Woman: Thanks. Now for the bad news. Harvard is not cheap. I nearly died when
5   I saw the tuition. I want to go, but I can't afford it. I already have four
6   years of undergrad loans at this school. If I do three years of Harvard
7   law, I'll be even more in debt. I'm not sure what to do.
8   Man: What about applying for a scholarship? How are your grades?
9   Woman: I'm _____ my class.
10   Man: There you go. You'd have a really good chance of getting a scholarship.
11   Some scholarships pay all your tuition. If you don't get a full scholarship,
12   you should at least get something for books. I got a scholarship here, and
13   boy did I save a bundle.
14   Woman: A scholarship is definitely _____ . I'll have to check it _____ .

1. a. accept	2. a. at the top	3. a. a hope	4. a. in
b. accepted	b. at the top of	b. a problem	b. off
c. accepted into	c. at the top in	c. an exit	c. up
d. expected at	d. at the top on	d. an option	d. out

11. Turmeric _____ the goddess of spice for good reason. As an antibacterial, it
     _____ infections; as an antioxidant, it _____ immune system; as an anti-
     inflammatory, it aids in digestion and protects against _____ .

1. a. is seen	2. a. fights	3. a. borrows the	4. a. arthritis
b. is called	b. finds	b. burns the	b. arrthritess
c. be called	c. fits	c. breaks the	c. arthreatise
d. will be called	d. fixes	d. boosts the	d. arhritis

12. One of the most famous battles of the War of 1812 was the Battle for Queenston Heights near Niagara Falls, Canada. The _____ Americans crossed the Niagara River and held the high ground at Queenston. The British, _____ general Sir Isaac Brock, charged up the heights and beat the Americans back; _____ , Brock, a rising star in the British army, _____ .

1. a. invasion	2. a. led by	3. a. moreover	4. a. was dead
b. invading	b. leaded by	b. thus	b. was killed
c. invaders	c. leded by	c. however	c. was done
d. inveighing	d. leded by	d. before that	d. was extinct

Notes

_____

_____

_____

_____

_____

_____

_____

_____

_____

_____

_____

_____

_____

_____

_____

_____

_____

_____

_____

_____

_____

_____

Written Expression → Exercise #8

<u>Task</u>: Identify the <u>3</u> errors in each passage. Check your answers on page 212.

1. <u>All sharks are carnivirous</u>. Some will eat just about anything. However, most
        A
    sharks are more selective, such as the whale shark, <u>which feed only on plank-</u>
                                                                B
    <u>ton</u>, microscopic organisms on the bottom of the ocean food chain. <u>The most</u>
                                                                                C
    feared shark <u>is the great white</u>. However, experts do not consider the great
                      D
    white to be the most dangerous. <u>That labell goes to the bull shark.</u>
                                            E

2. An algorithm is a process that performs a series of operations aimed at solving

    a problem. <u>More especially</u>, an algorithm has a starting point followed by a
                      A
    sequence of well-defined instructions <u>terminating at a end point</u>. Algorithms
                                                  B
    lie at the heart of computer software. Software, as you know, is basically a se-

    quence of instructions <u>aimed at carrying out a task</u>. That task is called a com-
                                  C
    putation. <u>It is a process that begins with a set of initial conditions</u>, called in-
                      D
    put, then provides an output, a result, <u>based on fixed set of</u> instructions.
                                                    E

3. <u>Archeologists agree that a major turning point in world history</u> was the ap-
                                  A
    pearance of literate civilizations in southwest Asia and along the Nile River.

    <u>This period date from about the fourth millennium BCE</u> to around 1,200
                                  B
    BCE. <u>Yet before we precede, we really need to define</u> the term civilization. With-
                  C
    in the word itself lies the root "civil" meaning to display the appropriate behav-

    ior. Yet this definition of civilization is far too broad, for what might be consid-

    ered appropriate behavior in one society <u>must be taboo in another</u>. Simply
                                                        D
    put, archeologists apply the term civilization by describing literate, urban-

    ized, state-level societies, the earliest <u>of which were city-states</u> in southwest
                                                      E
    Asia and along the Nile River.

4. <u>Ancient Egyptians use a formal writing system called hieroglyphs</u>. Hiero-
                                          A
glyphs combine logographic as well as alphabetic elements. For years, scholars

<u>were inable to decipher the meaning of hieroglyphs</u>. The Rosetta Stone
                          B
changed all that. In 1799, a French soldier, part of Napoleon's expedition to

Egypt, discovered it in a temple. <u>On it was a decree by King Ptolemy V</u> in en-
                                                  C
graved text. The decree is in three languages: Egyptian hieroglyphs, Egyptian

demotic script, and ancient Greek. Scholars who knew ancient Greek suddenly

had a means <u>of which they could finally translate hieroglyphs</u>. In 1801, the
                          D
British defeated the French in Egypt and the Rosetta Stone fell into British

hands, where it has remained ever since. This, then, has led to the debate

about who actually owns the Rosetta Stone, <u>a debate that persists to this day</u>.
                                                          E

5. <u>This may come as a surprise</u>, but hurricanes and tornadoes do not account for
      A
the most weather-related deaths in United States. <u>Heat and drought does</u>.
                                                          B
According to NOAA—the National Oceanographic <u>and</u> Atmospheric Administra-
                                                  C
tion—extreme heat is "<u>one of most underrated</u> and least understood of the
                          D
<u>dangerously weather phenomena</u>."
      E

6. <u>We've bin talking about preindustrial societies</u>, <u>which were agrarian-based</u>
                      A   B
with power concentrated in the hands of a king. <u>An industrial society, quiet</u>
                                                          C
<u>the contrary</u>, is one in which power and influence <u>is dispersed throughout</u>
                                                          D
<u>the society</u> and is based on fossil fuels, <u>whereby</u> preindustrial societies aren't.
                                                  E

7. The Roman Army was a highly disciplined and highly feared military force that,

by 300 BCE, had made the Republic of Rome <u>an unrivalled umpire controlling</u>
                                                          A
<u>eastern Europe and much of the Mediterranean</u>. The basic unit of the Roman

Army was the legion. <u>A legion was comprised of approximately 42,00 legion-</u>
                                          B

9
10 naires. These men, both professional and conscript, were each equipped with
11 three weapons: a pugio, a long dagger or knife, a gladius, a short thrusting
12
13 sword (from which the word "gladiator" is derived), and a pilum, a two-meter
14
15 javelin. With a shield for protection, and dressed in body armor, the legionnaire
16   C
17 was a killing machine. Imagine the terror the tribes of Europe felt when the
18   D
19 Roman army come marching toward them.
                                    E

1 8. A business plan has three main parts, starting with a formal statement that
2   A
3 outline a set of specific goals. Those goals will be either for profit or not-for
4
5 profit. A for-profit business plan will describe goals aimed at the creation of
6
7 wealth while a not-for profit business plan will focus on a mission statement
8   B
9 in order to receive tax exempt status from the government. Next, the business
10
11 plan will describe the reasons why the stated goal are attainable. Depending on
12   C
13 the plan, those reasons will be supported by a market analysis and a competi-
14
15 tor analysis, and whatever researches is necessary to attain the stated goal.
16   D
17 Finally, a business plan will state how the business will go about achieving
18
19 those goals. In other words, a plan of action. Let's begin by defining the first
20   E
21 part of a business plan: defining the goals.

1 9. A critical part of a marine biologist's research is to compill data by observing
2   A
3 events and by collecting samples. However, because the ocean is so vastly,
4   B
5 and because most of what is going on is happening below the waves, marine
6
7 biologists must devise ways to observe and collect samples. Some use nets and
8   C
9 dredges for gathering samples while others use computers for compiling data.
10
11 Still others they prefer experiments in labs designed to recreate specific ocean
12   D
13 environments. However, the best way, and frankly the only way to observe and
14

15   collect data, is <u>to get your feet wet</u>. In other words, you've got to enter the

16   E

17   ocean itself and see things with the naked eye.

1   10. <u>Herbalism is a traditional plant-based medicine</u>. It is also known as botanical

2   A

3   medicine, herbology, and phytotherapy. Herbalism has a long history stretch-

4

5   ing back <u>to the dawns of time</u>. Today, over 122 compounds used in modern

6   B

7   medicine <u>have been derived from plant sources</u>. Some of the more common

8   C

9   herbal medicines in use today are milk thistle, a thistle extract used for centu-

10

11   ries to maintain liver health, aloe vera, a traditional remedy for burns and

12

13   wounds, and willow bark, <u>a three bark extract the Greeks used</u> for aches and

14   D

15   pains, the main ingredient <u>of which has been synthesized into todays aspirin</u>.

                                                          E

Notes

_____

_____

_____

_____

_____

_____

_____

_____

_____

_____

_____

_____

_____

_____

_____

_____

Vocabulary → Exercise #8

Task: Choose the correct synonym. Check your answers on page 213.

1. innocuous (adj)

    a. harmless
    b. harmful
    c. harm
    d. harmed

2. burden (n)

    a. new issue
    b. fun idea
    c. small crime
    d. heavy load

3. avarice (n)

    a. goal
    b. greed
    c. wealth
    d. power

4. prospect (n)

    a. canned
    b. candied
    c. candid
    d. candidate

5. circumspect (adj)

    a. wonderful
    b. wary
    c. wise
    d. wishful

6. monarch (n)

    a. best friend
    b. co-worker
    c. new boss
    d. royal ruler

7. canard (n)

    a. false rumor
    b. good remedy
    c. old recipe
    d. right time

8. phobia (n)

    a. fear
    b. phantom
    c. desire
    d. idea

9. myriad (adj)

    a. few
    b. many
    c. some
    d. none

10. prolix (adj)

    a. wordy
    b. succinct
    c. balanced
    d. boring

11. assess (v)

    a. judge
    b. value
    c. contribute
    d. assassinate

12. polytheism (n)

    a. one god
    b. many gods
    c. no gods
    d. new gods

13. apt (adj)

    a. airy
    b. appropriate
    c. intelligent
    d. eager

14. inquiry (n)

    a. intelligence
    b. intrigue
    c. investment
    d. investigation

15. versatile (adj)

    a. many uses
    b. many issues
    c. many times
    d. many voices

16. prolific (adj)

    a. productive
    b. poor
    c. possible
    d. permissiable

17. concur (v)

    a. disagree
    b. agree
    c. agreeable
    d. agreed

18. discombobulated (adj)

    a. confused
    b. combined
    c. dislocated
    d. distant

Structure → Exercise #9

Task: Fill in the blanks with the correct answers. Check your answers on page 213.

1. A woodpecker is a _____ bird that hunts for _____ drilling its beak into the wood of a tree for insect larvae, an important food source for the bird. A hummingbird, _____ , searches for nectar inside flowers _____ long tongue.

1. a. flock of	2. a. food by	3. a. however	4. a. with the
b. species of	b. food on	b. therefore	b. with its
c. sort of	c. food in	c. as a result	c. with an
d. part of	d. food up	d. in contrast	d. with some

2. Wall Street is the financial center of the world. Many years ago there was an _____ wall. It _____ by Dutch settlers, the first _____ to settle on Manhattan Island in 1624. They built a wall around their settlement to protect themselves from Indians, who were growing more and more _____ .

1. a. actual	2. a. was delivered	3. a. Europe's	4. a. amicable
b. virtual	b. was bordered	b. Europeans	b. envious
c. ancient	c. was razed	c. Eurasians	c. hostile
d. invisible	d. was built	d. person	d. curious

3. _____ December 14, 1911, Norwegian _____ Roald Amundsen reached the South Pole. In so doing, he beat the British team headed by Robert Falcon Scott. _____ from the pole, Scott and his men, only twenty miles from base camp, succumbed to the _____ cold and died.

1. a. In	2. a. exploiter	3. a. Realizing	4. a. really
b. On	b. educator	b. Returning	b. warming
c. By	c. explorer	c. Repeating	c. changing
d. At	d. engineer	d. Revisiting	d. bitter

4. It is difficult _____ a top American university because the competition is very _____ . Moreover , you must demonstrate why you are good _____ academically but also how you have distinguished yourself outside of school, such as volunteering or _____ leader in your community.

1. a. to get in on	2. a. stiff	3. a. not ever	4. a. being
b. to get off with	b. malleable	b. not yet	b. be to
c. to get by on	c. forgiving	c. not but	c. to be a
d. to get into	d. intelligent	d. not just	d. being a

5. Aristotle _____ the greatest of the Greek philosophers. From him, we get the art of rhetoric, _____ how to argue persuasively and _____ audience that what you are arguing is right and good, and worth _____ .

	1.	2.	3.	4.
a.	is only	that is	convince a	considering
b.	is perhaps	which is	convince an	concerning
c.	is not	who is	convincing the	creating
d.	is was	how is	convince	combusting

6. Snakes have the ability _____ their skin. This process _____ molting. Birds also _____ . When they do, they lose their feathers. The purpose of molting is to make way _____ new skin or feathers.

	1.	2.	3.	4.
a.	to shed	is relieved	molt	before
b.	to delete	is believed	move	for
c.	to share	is made	masticate	to
d.	to grow	is called	manipulate	by

7. C. F. Martin has been _____ acoustic guitars since 1833 in Nazareth, Pennsylvania. Martins, _____ called, are considered _____ best acoustic guitars in the world. If your favorite musician is playing an acoustic guitar, _____ it is a Martin.

	1.	2.	3.	4.
a.	buttressing	as they are	to be one	chances are
b.	belittling	as it	to be an	seems it is
c.	crafting	as they	to be a	likely to be
d.	banishing	as you	to be the	able to do

8. Recently, it has been _____ that the American Chamber of Commerce—the largest association of businesses in America, representing every type of business from Microsoft _____ your local gas station owner—has been soliciting money from foreign corporations with U.S. operations, money _____ finding its way into the American political system regardless of what members of the Chamber of Commerce might think. Let's _____ the evidence.

	1.	2.	3.	4.
a.	remembered	down to	what is	look for
b.	regretted	over to	why is	look at
c.	realized	up to	where is	look
d.	revealed	beside of	which is	look to

9. All American companies have a social _____ called *a corporate ladder*. The boss is at the top of the ladder with everyone else below in _____ order of job importance. Even companies that are _____ , or claim to be egalitarian (Google, Apple, facebook), have distinct hierarchies. You can't see them, but the corporate ladders are there. The same _____ for educational institutions.

	1.	2.	3.	4.
a.	highlight	descending	family-fun	holds true
b.	homophone	amending	family-run	hold onto
c.	hierarchy	upending	family-friendly	hold off
d.	hiearchee	ascending	family-time	hold at

10. On December 7, 1941 Japanese _____ attacked the American Pacific naval fleet lying _____ in the safety of Pearl Harbor, Hawaii. The attack came at eight a.m., when the crews of the American ships were sleeping or at church. The Japanese carrier-borne planes _____ the Americans and destroyed the American Pacific Fleet. This action _____ America's entry into World War Two.

1. a. fight plains	2. a. on anchor	3. a. greeted	4. a. precipitated
b. fighter planes	b. at anchor	b. surprised	b. presumed
c. fitful flames	c. by anchor	c. perplexed	c. pressured
d. forceful aims	d. in anchor	d. captivated	d. purloined

Notes

_____

_____

_____

_____

_____

_____

_____

_____

_____

_____

_____

_____

_____

_____

_____

_____

_____

_____

_____

_____

Written Expression → Exercise #9

<u>Directions</u>: Identify <u>3</u> errors in each passage. Check your answers on page 214.

1. <u>A pitch is a argument designed</u> to deliver a product's unique selling proposi-
    A
    tion or USP. The USP defines the product's unique feature. The product could

    be a consumer item, <u>a corporate philosopher</u>, or you. The product's USP sets
    B
    the product apart from the competition. <u>This distinction creates value</u>. Value
    C
    is the perceived benefit of the product. The greater the product's distinction,

    the greater the product's value. The greater the value, <u>the greater the proba-</u>
    D
    <u>bility</u> people will be persuaded <u>to by the product you are pitching</u>.
    E

2. The Ku Klux Klan, a.k.a. the KKK or "the Klan," is a white supremacist organ-

    ization <u>founded in what was the southern states of American in 1860</u>. Its aim
    A
    was <u>to terrorize blacks freed in slavery</u>, for the Klan believed that the white
    B
    man was—and be would always—<u>the superior race</u>. Today, the Klan is much
    C
    smaller but still active. <u>Its neo-fascist views are ultra-nationalistic</u> and are
    D
    comparable to those of the Nazi party founded by Hitler in post-World War

    One Germany. <u>Many have accused Donald Trump of being the fascist</u>.
    E

3. <u>Imagine locking yourself in your bedroom and never coming out for years, or</u>
    A
    <u>not at all</u>. You have no friends. You eat fast food and talk to no one. <u>Your only</u>
    B
    <u>contact with the outside world is via the internet</u>. <u>You have no interest in</u>
    C
    <u>working, going to school, dating, or getting married</u>. You have rejected the out-

    side world and retreated into silence to read salacious comic books called

    manga. <u>These individuals, typically young Japanese males, they are called</u>
    D
    <u>"hikkomori" (heek-koh-moh-ree)</u>. The hikkomori phenomenon is a growing

    social and health crisis that accounts for one percent of the Japanese popula-

16   tion. Why are there so many hikkomori and what exactly is wrong with them?

17

18   Nobody knows. <u>But there are klues</u>.
                              E

1   4.   During the Prohibition Era in America, (1920 to 1933), most alcohol compa-

2

3   nies went out of business. <u>As a result, gangsters like Al Capone of Chicago,</u>

4   A

5   <u>moved in and started to control the flow of ellicit alcohol</u>. By today's stand-

6

7   ards, Capone made billions. <u>Albeit, he was famous for never being arrested</u>

8   B

9   despite his legendary track record of violence and corruption. However, Ca-

10

11   pone's <u>luck ran off</u> when, in 1927, the Supreme Court ruled that illegal

12   C

13   income was taxable. <u>On November 1931, in a Chicago courtroom, Al Capone</u>

14   D

15   <u>was convicted of tax evasion</u> and was sentenced to eleven years in prison,

16

17   much of which was spent in Alcatraz, the infamous island prison located in

18

19   the middle of San Francisco bay. Capone did his time and was released in

20

21   1939. <u>He died in 1947 in Miami of a sexually transmitted disease (STD)</u>.
                              E

1   5.   <u>The purpose of a formal product presentation is to persuade an audience to</u>

2   A

3   <u>buy the product you are pitching as a result it has value</u>. <u>A formal product</u>

4   B

5   <u>presentation pitches an idea in a controlling environment</u>, such as a confer-

6

7   ence room or meeting hall. This type of presentation is considered formal be-

8

9   cause: 1) <u>the presenter is assuming the roll of lecturer</u>; 2) <u>a lecturer is one</u>

10   C   D

11   <u>who argues formally before an audience</u>; 3) the audience is often sitting in a

12

13   formal arrangement, and; 4) the audience is often passive while the presenter

14

15   is active. <u>This active-passive hierarchy creates a formal atmosphere</u>.
                          E

6. <u>DNA typing, or profileing,</u> was developed by British scientist Sir Alec Jeffrys in
      A
the early 1980's. <u>It was originally used to be determine paternity, the genetic</u>
      B
<u>linking of a child with his or her parents.</u> <u>The results were so conclusive that</u>
      C
<u>DNA profiling quickly became an important tool</u> for the analysis of forensic
evidence gathered at crime scenes. <u>DNA was first enter into evidence in 1987</u>
      D
<u>in a UK murder trial.</u> Forensic investigators were able to identify the killer
<u>while exonerating the original suspect.</u>
      E

7. <u>The earliest writings were hard to read because they lacked punctuality.</u> In
      A
ancient Greece, for example, in order to understand a piece of writing, you
had to read it numerous times, especially if you were reading it out loud. It
wasn't until the third century BCE when Aristophanes of Byzantium, the head
librarian in the great library in Alexandria, <u>came up with the idea of inserting</u>
      B
<u>marks or dots to indicate</u> where to pause or end a passage. <u>Not everyone was</u>
      C
<u>on board with this idea.</u> <u>Cicero, the famous Roman orator, rejects the Greek</u>
      D
<u>system of punctuation,</u> as did most Romans thus the Greek system languished
<u>The raise of Christianity following the fall of Rome</u> reintroduced the Greek sys-
      E
tem.

8. Prior to 1500, the Indians of the Great Plains hunted buffalo on foot, a peri-
lous endeavor that often resulted in the death of more than one hunter. The
process began <u>with the entire village heading out for the hunt.</u> With a buffalo
      A
herd approaching—<u>and here we are talking about a million or more people</u>—
      B
the villagers would line up beside cairns, piles of rocks that <u>had been erected</u>
      C
<u>by previous hunters going back to prehistoric times.</u> The cairns acted as driv-
ing lanes that funneled the buffalo towards a cliff. <u>The villagers lined up off</u>
      D

15
16 both sides of the herd and, by waving blankets and skins, they would force

17
18 the buffalo into a stampede. Unable to stop, the buffalo would be forced to

19 jump off the cliff. This form of mass hunting it is called a buffalo jump.
                                                                    E

1 9. Later in life, when Charles Eames asked to explain his design philosophy,
2   A
3   he used what he called the banana leaf parable. In southern India, the broad
4   B
5   flat banana leave is used as a base for food, much like a plate or dish. Accord-
6
7   ing to Charles Eames, the banana leaf is the foundation from which ideas
8
9   grow. In other words, when designing, the Eames always imagined the banana
10   C
11   leave, a natural design that is simple, functional and affordable. Any ideas
12
13   that developed from the banana leaf, the original basic idea, had to reflect the
14
15   simplicity, the functionality, and the affordability of the banana leaf itself. The
16   D
17   genius of Charles and Ray Eames' work is a testement to the banana leaf par-
18   E
19   able.

1 10. Résumé writing, like all business correspondence, is a step-by-step process.
2   A
3   For a résumé, that process begins with defining the type of job you seek. The
4
5   job market is hierarchal by nature. Your work experience and education will
6   B
7   define where you stand on the job latter and the type of job you seek. For ex-
8
9   ample, college grads generally seek entry-level jobs. These jobs are on the low-
10
11   er end of the job ladder. Professionals, similarly, will seek positions com-
12   C
13   mensurate with their experience. These jobs are higher up the job ladder.
14
15   Once you know your position in the job ladder, and the type of job you seek,
16   D
17   you must decide which type of résumé to write: targeted or non-targeted.
                            E

Vocabulary → Exercise #9

Task: Choose the correct synonym. Check your answers on page 214.

1. apologist (n)

   a. one who asks
   b. one who defends
   c. one who analyzes
   d. one who apologizes

2. volcanologist (n)

   a. can expert
   b. vole expert
   c. cane expert
   d. volcano expert

3. criminologist (n)

   a. criminal expert
   b. money expert
   c. building expert
   d. car expert

4. musicologist (n)

   a. illness expert
   b. music expert
   c. business expert
   d. muscle expert

5. ornithologist (n)

   a. bird expert
   b. echo expert
   c. special expert
   d. cooking expert

6. lexicologist (n)

   a. word expert
   b. MS Word expert
   c. dictionary expert
   d. TOEFL expert

7. neurologist (n)

   a. European doctor
   b. new doctor
   c. brain doctor
   d. skin doctor

8. primatologist (n)

   a. prison expert
   b. primate expert
   c. personal expert
   d. pet expert

9. virologist (n)

   a. hacker expert
   b. computer expert
   c. virtual expert
   d. virus expert

10. oncologist (n)

    a. arm doctor
    b. heart doctor
    c. cancer doctor
    d. therapy doctor

11. zoologist (n)

    a. animal expert
    b. zoo expert
    c. training expert
    d. hospital expert

12. phonologist (n)

    a. vocal sound expert
    b. local sound expert
    c. audio sound expert
    d. vision sound expert

13. mixologist (n)

    a. alcoholic expert
    b. mixed menu expert
    c. mixed drink expert
    d. mixed up expert

14. cardiologist (b)

    a. car expert
    b. heart doctor
    c. cardigan expert
    d. hearth expert

15. climatologist (n)

    a. climate expert
    b. material expert
    c. climbing expert
    d. independent expert

16. seismologist (n)

    a. earthquake expert
    b. systems expert
    c. isthmus expert
    d. novel expert

17. glaciologist (n)

    a. glacier expert
    b. river expert
    c. snow expert
    d. water expert

18. dermatologist (n)

    a. skin doctor
    b. dental expert
    c. eye expert
    d. foot expert

<u>Structure</u> → **Exercise #10**

<u>Task</u>: Fill in the blanks with the correct answers. Check your answers on page 215.

1. "I'm selfish, impatient and a little _____ . I make mistakes; I am out of control and at times hard to _____ . But if you can't handle me at my _____ , then you sure...don't _____ me at my best."

   — Marilyn Monroe

1. a. inimical	2. a. handle	3. a. worst	4. a. deride
b. inscrutable	b. harbor	b. wit	b. debunk
c. insincere	c. hawk	c. wisdom	c. desire
d. insecure	d. heal	d. waning	d. deserve

2. "Power is of two kinds. One is _____ the fear of punishment and the other by _____ . Power based on love is a thousand times more _____ and permanent than the one _____ from fear of punishment."

   — Mahatma Gandhi

1. a. abstained by	2. a. ideas of love	3. a. invective	4. a. derived
b. attained by	b. acts of love	b. objective	b. deranged
c. obtained by	c. of love	c. effective	c. debated
d. refrained by	d. events	d. reflective	d. defeated

3. "All the world's _____ , and all the men and women _____ players. They have their exits and their _____ ; and one man in his _____ plays many parts."

   — William Shakespeare, *As You Like It* (Act II, Scene VII)

1. a. a slave	2. a. merely	3. a. entreaties	4. a. treatment
b. a stage	b. moistly	b. enticements	b. time
c. a sieve	c. wisely	c. entrances	c. testimony
d. a siege	d. meekly	d. enmities	d. trembling

4. "I am tired and _____ war. Its glory is all moonshine. It is only for those who have neither fired a shot nor heard the shrieks _____ of the wounded who cry aloud for blood, for _____ , for desolation. War is _____ ."

   — William Tecumseh Sherman, Union general, American Civil War, 1861-1865

1. a. know of	2. a. and groans	3. a. victory	4. a. heaven
b. need of	b. and grinding	b. veracity	b. hell
c. think of	c. and goading	c. veneration	c. inspiring
d. sick of	d. and giving	d. vengeance	d. eternal

5. "All _____ passes through three stages. First, it is _____ . Second, it is violently _____ . Third, it is accepted as being _____ ."

— Arthur Schopenhauer

1. a. tenets	2. a. rectified	3. a. accepted	4. a. self-centered
b. tentacles	b. redesigned	b. calibrated	b. self-denial
c. testing	c. ridiculed	c. opposed	c. self-evident
d. truth	d. realigned	d. masticated	d. self-effacing

1
2
3
4
5
6
7
8

6. "Man cannot survive except through his mind. He comes on earth _____ . His brain is his only weapon. Animals obtain food by force. Man had no claws, no fangs, no horns, no great strength of _____ . He must plant his food or hunt it. To plant, he needs a process of thought. To hunt, he needs weapons, and to make weapons a process of thought. From this simplest necessity to the highest religious _____ , from the wheel to the skyscraper, everything we are and have comes from a single attribute of man—the function of his _____ mind."

— Ayn Rand, *The Fountainhead*

1. a. unattached	2. a. muscle	3. a. abstraction	4. a. rejoicing
b. untested	b. memory	b. ceremony	b. regressive
c. unarmed	c. mirth	c. situation	c. recalcitrant
d. unrepentant	d. mythology	d. sarcasm	d. reasoning

7. "_____ not listen to those who think we ought to be angry with our enemies, and who believe this to be great and _____ . Nothing is so praiseworthy, nothing so clearly shows a great and _____ soul, as clemency and readiness to _____ ."

— Marcus Tullius Cicero

1. a. Praise us	2. a. manly	3. a. navigating	4. a. forgive
b. Teach us	b. maligned	b. nourishing	b. forgo
c. Let us	c. munificent	c. nostalgic	c. forsake
d. Free us	d. mendacious	d. noble	d. forestall

1
2
3
4
5
6

8. "Before I go on with this short _____ , let me make a general observation: the test of a first-rate intelligence is the ability to hold two opposed ideas in the mind at the same time, and still _____ the ability to function. One should, for example, be able to see that things are hopeless and yet be determined to make them otherwise. This _____ fitted on to my early adult life, when I saw the improbable, the implausible, often the "impossible," _____ ."

— F. Scott Fitzgerald, *The Crack-Up*

1. a. bombast	2. a. remain	3. a. philosophy	4. a. come true
b. history	b. restrain	b. philandering	b. come close
c. diatribe	c. retain	c. phrasing	c. come to not
d. screed	d. relinquish	d. fantasizing	d. come to heel

1   9.   "Men _____ thought as they fear nothing else on earth—more than ruin,
2   more even than death. Thought is subversive and revolutionary, destructive
3   and terrible, thought is merciless to privilege, _____ institutions, and com-
4   fortable habits; thought is anarchic and lawless, indifferent to authority, care-
5   less of the well-tried wisdom of the _____ . Thought looks into the pit of hell
6   and is not afraid...Thought is great and swift and free, the light of the world,
7   and the chief _____ of man."

— Bertrand Russell, *Why Men Fight*

1. a. shirk	2. a. established	3. a. anarchists	4. a. aim
b. welcome	b. estranged	b. apologists	b. failing
c. fear	c. estrogenic	c. apes	c. glooming
d. ignore	d. esoteric	d. ages	d. glory

10.   "It's been proven by quite a few studies that plants are good for our _____ development. If you _____ an area, the rate of _____ goes down. Torture _____ recover when they spend time outside in a garden with flowers."

— Jane Goodall

1. a. chemical	2. a. grow	3. a. crime	4. a. victims
b. cosmological	b. grate	b. growing	b. protestors
c. psychological	c. green	c. development	c. plaintiffs
d. philosophical	d. grind	d. helping	d. vessels

Notes

_____

_____

_____

_____

_____

_____

_____

_____

_____

_____

_____

_____

Written Expression → Exercise #10

<u>Task</u>: Identify the <u>4</u> errors in each passage. The errors are indicated four of the six letters. Check your answers on page 215.

1. Chemotherapy (or chemo) is a type of cancer treatment. Chemo drugs are

    used <u>alone and in combination with other drugs to combat cancer</u>. Chemo
    A

    drugs <u>are designed to destroy new cells</u>. Because cancer cells grow quickly,
    B

    chemo drugs target these cells with the aim of interrupting the cell cycle. By

    doing so, chemo drugs stop the development and spread of cancerous cells.

    That is the good news. The bad news <u>is the chemo drug can't distinguish be-</u>
    C

    <u>tween cancer's cells and healthy cells</u>. The healthy <u>cells effected are the blood-</u>
    D

    <u>forming cells in the bones</u>, hair follicles (leading to a loss of hair), and cells in

    the mouth, digestive tract, and reproductive system. The destruction of

    healthy cells can result in the patient feeling weak and tired. Such a weak-

    ened state means <u>the patients immune system is at risk of contracting other</u>
    E

    <u>diseases</u>, such as colds. Doctor's will then prescribe a regimen of antibiotics

    plus other drugs <u>to combat the side affects of chemo, such as nausea</u>.
    F

2. There is a great variety of Indian houses. Wigwams are small, wooden houses

    built by the Algonquins, <u>Indians indigenous to the forests of eastern Canadian,</u>
    A

    <u>particularly Quebec</u>. The walls of a wigwam are made of woven mats of birch-

    bark supported by frames made of small tree trunks. The frame is typically

    shaped into a doom, a cone or a rectangle. <u>Once the exterior mats are in</u>
    B

    <u>place, they are secured by stripes of wood and rope</u>. Wigwams are not trans-

    portable yet are fast and easy to build, and offer a safe and secure shelter

    against the harsh Canadian winter. <u>Because of their small size</u>, a wigwam
    C

    housed only one family. The Iroquois, the Algonquin's southern neighbors

18
19
20
21
22
23
24
25
26
27
28
29
30
31
32
33
34
35
36
37
38

in the northeastern United States, built longhouses. Longhouses are essen-

tially big wigwams. History records some longhouses as long as two-hundred

feet. <u>Inside, along the walls, raised platforms served as beds</u> while screens di-
                                    D

vided the space into private compartments. A longhouse was home to a clan, a

group of people within the tribe related by blood. Six clans residing in a

longhouse was not unusual. The western plains Indians, such as the Sioux

and Cheyenne, were hunters. <u>By following the buffalo, they had a ready meat</u>
                                                    E

<u>supply</u>. It also meant that the Indians were always on the move. Their primary

dwelling, the teepee, was designed to accommodate the plains Indian's noma-

dic life. <u>The teepee is a tall, cone-shape tent covered with buffalo skins with</u>
                                            F

<u>an opening at the top for smoke</u>.

1
2
3
4
5
6
7
8
9
10
11
12
13
14
15
16
17

3. There are two types of earthquake: <u>convergent, transform, and divergent</u>. A
                                                    A

convergent earthquake, or dip slip earthquake, <u>occurs when one part of the</u>
                                                        B

<u>earth moves up and another moves down</u> along a crack in the ground called a

fault. <u>A transformative earthquake, or strike-slip quack</u>, occurs when the
                            C

earth along a fault moves horizontally. One side of a fault moves east while

the other moves west. A divergent quake <u>occurs when the ground seperates</u>.
                                                        D

Divergent quakes <u>are common at the ocean floor</u>. The San Francisco earth
                        E

quake of 1906 was strike slip earthquake while the Indian Ocean earthquake

of 2012 <u>was a dip-slip</u> earthquake.
              F

4. At 29,029 feet (8,849 meters), Mountain Everest is <u>the highest mountain of the</u>
    A
    <u>world</u>. <u>It was first climbed in 1953</u> by New Zealander Sir Edmund Hillary with
    B
    the help of his Nepalese Sherpa Tensing Norgay. Today, Everest is a popular

    destination <u>for intrepid climbers</u> seeking <u>the more coveted prize</u> in the sport of
    C   D
    mountaineering. <u>However, descending Everest is not without peril</u>. To reach
    E
    the top, climbers must use oxygen in the area known as the Death Zone. The

    Death Zone is littered with over two-hundred dead and frozen climbers, a griz-

    zly reminder that humans <u>are not built to life at the cruising altitude of a</u>
    F
    <u>passenger jet</u>.

5. Typically, <u>when coffee is grown</u>, all surrounding non-coffee trees and bushes
    A
    <u>are cut down to allow more sun light or rain</u> to reach the coffee plants. Not
    B
    so with shade-grown coffee. Growers <u>of this coffee type</u> are aware that protect-
    C
    ing local fauna is important, especially birds, <u>to need these same trees and</u>
    D
    <u>bushes to build nests</u>. Knowing this, growers of shade-grown coffee <u>do cut</u>
    E
    <u>down endemic fauna</u> and instead grow their coffee plants in the shade of

    these same bushes and trees. The result is shade-grown coffee <u>that is both</u>
    F
    <u>delicious and echo-friendly</u>.

6. <u>An invasive species is an organism who has found a new home in a new land</u>.
    A
    The brown snake, for example, arrived in Guam by ship <u>shortly after the</u>
    B
    <u>World War Two</u> and has since wreaked havoc on <u>the local wildelife population</u>.
    C
    So far, the introduction of the brown snake <u>has resulted in the extinction of</u>
    D
    <u>twelve bird species once native to Guam</u>. The cane toad has done the same in

    Australia. A native of South and Central America, the cane toad was intro-

    duced into Australia as a form of natural agricultural pest to control beetles

15 eating sugarcane fields. <u>The cane toad failed to do so yet bred rapidly</u>.
16   E
17 Worse, with its voracious appetite, it soon became a pest itself, eating every-
18
19 thing that comes it way, <u>including birds, mouses, and small reptiles</u>. More-
20   F
21 over, because it is poisonous, local predator populations have declined due to
22
23 poisoning upon ingesting cane toads.

1   7. Parrots are so smart, researchers call them "feathered primates." Primates,
2
3   <u>such as chimpanzees and gorillas</u>, are famous for their intelligence. Their abil-
4   A
5   ity to problem solve, and to make tools <u>to aid in food-gaddering</u>, is well docu-
6   B
7   mented. <u>This intelligence is also finded in parrots</u>. Moreover, they communi-
8   C
9   cate in their own dialects, <u>are skilled with the numbers</u>, and are quite adapta-
10   D
11   ble. Monk parakeets from South America, for example, <u>are thriving in New</u>
12   E
13   <u>York City</u> while lilac-crowned Amazons <u>have escaped and are doing quit well</u>
14   F
15   <u>in Los Angeles</u>.

1   8. Symbiosis occurs <u>when two organs are mutually supportive</u>, such as fruit
2   A
3   bats and fruit trees. While eating fruit, fruit bats benefit from the fruit's nutri-
4
5   tional value <u>while, at the same time, consuming the seeds within the fruit</u>.
6   B
7   These digested seeds are then dispersed and fertilized as the bats excrete
8
9   them. By doing so, <u>bats are helping to generation new fruit trees</u>. This is
10   C
11   good for fruit trees, bats, and the environment as a whole. Granivory, or seed
12
13   predation, in contrast, <u>ocurs when an organism eats seeds</u>. The result is the
14   D
15   seeds are completely digested <u>and can no longer be germanated</u>. Humans,
16   E
17   insects, and birds <u>are the most common granivores</u>.
                                  F

9. <u>Sibling ribalry occurs</u> when offspring <u>fight for dominance and survial</u>. Bald-
   A   B
eagle chicks are a good example. The mother eagle will produce two or three

eggs, which hatch into eaglets around the middle of March. The chicks grow

fast and demand <u>a constantly supply of food</u>, <u>what their parents provide</u>. As
                 C   D
the chicks compete for food, the stronger one <u>will push the weaker one</u>
                                               E
<u>aside</u> and dominate the nest. <u>As a result</u>, the weaker sibling dies. Cruel as it
                                F
might seem, sibling rivalry ensures that the strongest of the species survives.

10. <u>Today, wearing pants is no big deal, for men and woman alike</u>. However, it
    A
was not always the case for women. In America, prior to 1851, women were

expected <u>to wear dresses that were long and not very practicable</u>, especially
          B
when it came to work. Also, the fashion of the day dictated that women wear

corsets, a type of girdle <u>drawn tight around the waist</u>. Back then, narrow
                          C
waists were all the rage; however, they were also a health risk too, not to men-

tion uncomfortable. <u>On top in that</u>, women wore undergarments called petti-
                     D
cots that, when layered, weighed as much as ten pounds. But that was the

norm. One woman, however, was not interested in satisfying conventional

tastes. Her name was Elizabeth Miller Smith. Smith, an early feminist and

social reformer, was born into a rich, progressive New York family, who intro-

duced her to new ideas and often took her traveling abroad. <u>In 1851</u>, while in
                                                             E
Turkey, Smith adopted the Turkish custom of wearing pantaloons, comforta-

ble pants that were wide and baggy. <u>Smith brought Turkey pantaloons back</u>
                                     F
<u>to the U.S. and started wearing them under short dresses thus becoming</u>

<u>the first woman in the United States to wear pants</u>. Her friend and fellow re-

formist, Amelia Bloom, took the idea and designed "bloomers," short, loose-

fitting, knee-length undergarments that became all the rage.

Vocabulary → Exercise #10

Task: Choose the correct synonym. Check your answers on page 216.

1. acrophobia (n)

   a. fear of fun
   b. fear of dogs
   c. fear of alcohol
   d. fear of heights

2. agliophobia (n)

   a. fear of smells
   b. fear of people
   c. fear of meat
   d. fear of pain

3. cynophobia (n)

   a. fear of cats
   b. fear of rats
   c. fear of dogs
   d. fear of camels

4. bibliophobia (n)

   a. fear of brains
   b. fear of books
   c. fear of beer
   d. fear of bread

5. ophidiophobia (n)

   a. fear of snakes
   b. fear of bears
   c. fear birds
   d. fear of turtle

6. lygophobia (n)

   a. fear of light
   b. fear of the dark
   c. fear of string
   d. fear of ridicule

7. suriphobia (n)

   a. fear of bicycles
   b. fear of rats
   c. fear of mice
   d. fear of heat

8. tachophobia (n)

   a. fear of money
   b. fear of Satan
   c. fear of speed
   d. fear of phones

9. pteromerhanophoiba (n)

   a. fear of batteries
   b. fear of knives
   c. fear of pteros
   d. fear of flying

10. nosocomephobia (n)

    a. fear of apartments
    b. fear of offices
    c. fear of cafes
    d. fear of hospitals

11. bacillophobia (n)

    a. fear of microbes
    b. fear of plants
    c. fear of snow
    d. fear of hands

12. aichmophobia (n)

    a. fear of fire
    b. fear of clowns
    c. fear of doctors
    d. fear of needles

13. phasmophobia (n)

    a. fear of angels
    b. fear of Satan
    c. fear of ghosts
    d. fear of churches

14. entomophobia (b)

    a. fear of cats
    b. fear of insects
    c. fear of forests
    d. fear of dirt

15. pentheraphobia (n)

    a. fear of mother-in-law
    b. fear of son-in-law
    c. fear of father-in-law
    d. fear of parents

16. tropophobia (n)

    a. fear of change
    b. fear of love
    c. fear of god
    d. fear of thunder

17. coulrophobia (n)

    a. fear of clowns
    b. fear of kings
    c. fear of snow
    d. fear of germs

18. pocrescophobia (n)

    a. fear of gaining weight
    b. fear of wealth
    c. fear of thinking
    d. fear of TOEFL

Answer Key and Tape Scripts

Part I – Argument Strategies

Pg. 18   Exercise #1: Rhetorical Strategies → Level 1

1. Bananas are grown in both tropical and sub-tropical zones.

    illustration: bananas; tropical and sub-tropical zones;
    description: tropical zone, sub-tropical zone;
    CC: tropical vs. sub-tropical zones;
    CE: plant bananas in tropical and sub-tropical zones and they grow.

2. Maria has always been a hard worker unlike her brother who is lazy.

    illustration: Mary; Mary's brother;
    description: Mary is hard working, brother is lazy;
    CC: hard-working Mary vs lazy brother;
    CE: give Mary a job and she will do it; give brother a job and he won't do it.

3. Yesterday was so cold that my car wouldn't start, but my wife's started no problem.

    illustration: my car; my wife's car;
    description: yesterday was so cold;
    CC: my car not starting vs. my wife's car starting;
    CE: when I tried to start my car, it did not start; when my wife tried to start her car, it started.

4. Canada is bigger than the United States but smaller than Russia.

    illustration: Canada, United States, Russia;
    description: Canada is bigger than the United States but smaller than Russia;
    CC: Canada vs. United States; Canada vs. Russia.

5. "The early bird gets the worm" is a popular idiom that means hard work will eventually pay off.

    illustration: "The early bird gets the worm" = example of a popular idiom;
    definition: "The early bird gets the worm" is a popular idiom that means hard work will eventually pay off;
    CE: get up early and work hard, and you will be rewarded with success; those who do not get up early and work hard will not succeed;
    CC: winners vs. losers.

6. After I got home, I made a late dinner, watched TV, then went to bed. I got up at seven a.m., showered, then met my best friend for an early breakfast.

    illustration: I (the writer); best friend; early breakfast;

narration: After I got home...made dinner...watched TV...went to bed...got up at seven a.m.,...showered, then met best friend;
description: late dinner; watched TV; seven a.m.; best friend; showered; early breakfast;

7. At the organic store, you can buy long grain rice, medium grain, and short grain.

   illustration: organic store; rice;
   description: organic store; long grain rice, medium grain rice, short grain rice;
   CC: long grain rice vs. medium grain rice vs. short grain rice;
   classification: long grain rice, medium grain rice, short grain rice.

8. Last year, Al traveled to Japan, Iran, Turkey, and Latvia but not Taiwan.

   illustration: Al; Japan, Iran, Turkey, Latvia, Taiwan;
   description: last year;
   CC: Al traveled to Japan, Iran, Turkey and Latvia but not Taiwan.

9. If you want to study in the United States, you must get a student visa.

   illustration: student visa; United States;
   description: student visa; if you want to study;
   CE: If you want to study in the United States, you must get a student visa.

10. Eva is a shopaholic. She loves to buy French shoes, Italian handbags and American designer jeans. However, she loves buying hats most of all.

    illustration: Eva; French shoes; Italian handbags; American designer jeans;
    description: Eva is a shopaholic; French shoes, Italian handbags, American designer jeans; she loves buying hats most of all;
    CC: buying French shoes, Italian handbags, American designer jeans vs. buying hats; loves hats more than shoes, handbags, and jeans;
    CE: When Eva goes shopping, she spends a lot of money.

11. In China, killing the endangered panda, an animal that eats only bamboo, is punishable by death.

    illustration: China; panda;
    description: in China; endangered panda; eats only bamboo; punishable by death;
    CE: killing a panda is punishable by death.

12. Four sitting American presidents have been assassinated: Lincoln (1865), Garfield (1881), McKinley (1901), and Kennedy (1963).

    illustration: Lincoln (1865), Garfield (1881), McKinley (1901), Kennedy (1963);
    description: four sitting American presidents; assassinated;
    CC: Lincoln (1865) vs. Garfield (1881) vs. McKinley (1901) vs. Kennedy (1963).

13. An eight-ounce glass of milk has eight grams of protein, whereas a similar glass of almond milk contains one gram of protein.

   illustration: a glass of milk; a glass of almond milk;
   description: an eight-ounce glass of milk has eight grams of protein; a similar glass of almond milk contains one gram of protein;
   CC: the protein in an eight-ounce glass of milk vs. the protein in an eight-ounce glass of almond milk; milk protein vs. almond milk protein; eight grams of protein vs one gram of protein;
   CE: drink milk and get more protein than a similar glass of almond milk.

14. A pro-con debate is an argument in which two or more people support opposing sides of an issue, for example, gun control in America.

   illustration: a pro-con debate; gun control in America;
   definition: a pro-con debate is an argument in which two or more people support opposing sides of an issue, for example, gun control in America;
   description: pro-con debate; two or more people; opposing sides; gun control in America.
   CC: pro vs. con; two or more people support opposing sides of an issue.

15. Coca Cola, the world's most popular soft drink, was invented in 1886. It was originally sold as medicine to increase brain and muscle power.

   illustration: Coca Cola;
   description: world's most popular soft drink; was invented in 1886; originally sold as medicine; brain and muscle power;
   CE: drink Coke in 1886, increase your brain and muscle power;
   CC: original Coke sold as medicine vs. Coke now sold as a soft drink.

Pg. 19   Exercise #2: Rhetorical Strategies → Level 2

1 1. The Emperor penguin is the largest penguin in the world, standing on average 45
2   inches tall. To survive the harsh Antarctic winters, they huddle together for
3   warmth. This cooperative behavior is unique in the animal world. The female gives
4   birth to one egg, then leaves it behind with the male as she goes off in search of
5   food. Food is in the ocean, often a 30-mile walk from the rookery.

   illustration: Emperor penguin; cooperative behavior;
   description: largest penguin; 45-inches tall; cooperative behavior is unique;
   harsh Antarctic winters; one egg; 30-mile walk to ocean; rookery;
   CE: female gives birth to one egg, then leaves it behind as she goes off in search of food; to survive, they huddle together for warmth;
   CC: female role vs. male role.

1 2. Diabetes is one of the most common diseases in the world today. Yet few know
2   who discovered insulin, the drug that helps patients fight diabetes. Insulin was
3   discovered by Canadian doctors Frederick Banting and Charles H. Best in 1921.
4   They extracted insulin from the pancreas of a healthy dog, then injected it into a

5   dog suffering from diabetes. The sick dog recovered. With the help of chemists
6   J.J.R. Macleod and James Collip, they developed human insulin. They tested it on
7   a diabetic boy close to death and he miraculously recovered. In 1923, Best and
8   MacLeod won the Nobel Prize for medicine. However, controversy ensued. Banting
9   believed that Best and Collip were overlooked by the committee.

illustration: diabetes; sick dog; sick boy; Banting, Best, Macleod, Collip;
description: one of the most common diseases today; ...insulin, the drug that
helps patients fight diabetes; Canadian doctors Frederick Banting and Charles
H. Best; sick dog; healthy dog; human insulin; diabetic boy;
CC: common disease yet few know who discovered insulin; sick vs healthy dog;
boy close to death vs. boy who recovers; Best and MacLeod won the Nobel Prize for
medicine. However, controversy ensued. Banting believed that Best and Collip
were overlooked by the committee;
process: They (Banting and Best) extracted insulin from the pancreas of a
healthy dog, then injected it into a dog suffering from diabetes. The sick dog recovered;
CE: ...injected it into a dog suffering from diabetes, the sick dog recovered; they
tested (insulin) on a diabetic boy close to death and he miraculously recovered;
Best and MacLeod (discovered insulin) won the Nobel Prize for medicine;
narration: Insulin was discovered by Canadian doctors Frederick Banting and
Charles H. Best in 1921; in 1923, Best and MacLeod won the Nobel Prize for
medicine.

1   3.   Inventory is a business word that describes the total amount of goods and/or ma-
2   terial a company has on hand. Taking inventory means counting those goods and
3   material. Taking inventory is an essential business practice. Factory owners need
4   to know how many finished products are available for sale and if they have the
5   parts and material to build those products. Car dealers often have high inventory.
6   To move their old inventory, they often have sales, particularly at the end of the
7   year when new car models are arriving.

definition: Inventory is a business word that describes the total amount of goods
and/or material a company has on hand;
description: business word; essential business practice; finished products; car
dealers; high inventory; old inventory; business word; factory owners; new car
models;
CC: old inventory vs. new inventory;
illustration: car dealers;
CE: to move their old inventory, (car dealers) often have sales.

1   4.   The hierarchy of Latin honors describes three levels of student achievement.
2   First is cum laude, which means "with honor." Next is magna cum laude. It means
3   "with great honor." The highest honor is summa cum laude. It means "with the
4   highest praise." A "summa" is a student who has demonstrated academic excel-
5   lence and is at the top of his or her class. Barack Obama graduated magna cum
6   laude from Harvard Law School. Natalie Portman graduated magna cum laude
7   from the University of Pennsylvania while the rapper Ludacris graduated summa
8   cum laude in business from Georgia State University.

classification: The hierarchy of Latin honors describes three levels of student

achievement: cum laude, magna cum laude, summa cum laude;
definition: The hierarchy of Latin honors describes three levels of student achievement: cum laude, magna cum laude, summa cum laude;
description: Cum laude...means "with honor"; "magna cum laude"...means "with great honor"; "summa cum laude" [means] a student who has demonstrated academic excellence and is at the top of his or her class;
illustration: Barack Obama graduated magna cum laude from Harvard Law School; Natalie Portman graduated magna cum laude from the University of Pennsylvania; the rapper Ludacris graduated summa cum laude in business from Georgia State University.

1   5.   Tea, an aromatic beverage made from the cured leaves of the Camelia Sinensis
2   plant, is the most widely consumed beverage in the world with coffee gaining in
3   popularity. Of the two, tea offers the greatest health benefits. A cup of black tea is
4   filled with anti-oxidants and cancer-fighting compounds, whereas a Harvard study
5   revealed that coffee has no health benefits. Of the two, coffee is higher in caffeine
6   while neither offers any nutritional value.

illustration: tea (Camelia Sinensis);
definition: tea, an aromatic beverage made from the cured leaves of the Camelia Sinensis plant;
CC: tea is the most widely consumed beverage in the world with coffee gaining in popularity; tea offers the greatest health benefits; a cup of black tea is filled with anti-oxidants and cancer-fighting compounds whereas a Harvard study revealed that coffee has no health benefits; coffee is higher in caffeine while neither offers any nutritional value;
description: (tea) most widely consumed beverage; greatest health benefits; a cup of black tea is filled with anti-oxidants and cancer-fighting compounds; a Harvard study; coffee is higher in caffeine;
CE: a Harvard study revealed that coffee has no health benefits; neither (tea nor coffee) offers any nutritional value.

Pg. 20   Exercise #3: Rhetorical Strategies → Level 3

1   1.   The animal kingdom is comprised of cold and warm-blooded animals. The body
2   temperature of cold-blooded or ectothermic animals is regulated by the external
3   environment while internal mechanisms keep the body temperature of warm-
4   blooded or endothermic animals constant. Reptiles, such as lizards and snakes,
5   are cold-blooded whereas mammals, such as whales and humans, are warm-
6   blooded. Most animals are warm-blooded; however, there are exceptions, such as
7   bats and moles. Their body temperatures vary depending on whether or not they
8   are active. Because warm-blooded animals generate body heat internally, they
9   must eat 10 times more than cold-blooded animals. As a result, warm-blooded an-
10   imals must be capable of finding food to meet this need. On the other hand, be-
11   cause cold-blood animals are heated by the sun's energy, they require less food.

description: animal kingdom; cold-blooded, or ectothermic, animals; external environment; internal mechanisms; warm-blooded, or endothermic, animals;
CC: cold vs. warm-blooded animals; the body temperature of cold-blooded, or ectothermic, animals is regulated by the external environment while internal

mechanisms keep the body temperature of warm-blooded, or endothermic, animals constant; reptiles, such as lizards and snakes, are cold-blooded whereas mammals, such as whales and humans, are warm-blooded; because warm-blooded animals generate body heat internally, they must eat 10 times more than cold-blooded animals vs. because cold-blood animals are heated by the sun's energy, they require less food;

illustration: animal kingdom; reptiles, lizards, snakes; mammals, whales, humans; bats, moles;

CE: because warm-blooded animals generate body heat internally, they must eat 10 times more than cold-blooded animals. As a result, warm-blooded animals must be capable of finding food to meet this need; because cold-blood animals are heated by the sun's energy, they require less food.

2. 1 Cloning is the process of making an exact copy of an original organism through
    2 asexual reproduction using one parent, whereas reproduction consists of two par-
    3 ents, a male and a female. The most famous cloned animal was Dolly the sheep
    4 however Dolly was not an exact replica of her parent. Genetic material from the
    5 donor cell into which Dolly's parents' DNA had to be inserted was .01 %. To clone
    6 Dolly, it took 277 donor eggs and 29 embryos before birth was achieved. Humans
    7 can be cloned; however, that idea remains controversial. Many believe it is unethi-
    8 cal to harvest human donor eggs and experiment with embryos. Cloning extinct
    9 animals, such as the wooly mammoth, however has gained popularity in recent
    10 years. Yet this too has raised serious issues, for bringing back extinct animals
    11 could drastically alter the natural order, especially if the animal cloned were a T-
    12 Rex.

    definition: Cloning is the process of making an exact copy of an original organism through asexual reproduction using one parent;

    CC: cloning is the process of making an exact copy of an original organism through asexual reproduction using one parent, whereas reproduction consists of two parents, a male and a female;

    illustration: the most famous cloned animal was Dolly the sheep; T-Rex;

    description: exact copy; original organism; the most famous cloned animal; asexual reproduction; two parents; not an exact replica of her parent; genetic material; controversial; extinct animals; wooly mammoth; serious issues; natural order; T-Rex;

    CE: to clone Dolly, it took 277 donor eggs and 29 embryos before birth was achieved; humans can be cloned; many believe it is unethical to harvest donor eggs and to experiment with embryos and eggs; cloning extinct animals, such as the wooly mammoth, however, has gained popularity in recent years; bringing back extinct animals could drastically alter the natural order.

3. 1 Her name was Norma Jeane Baker. The world knew her as the movie star Marilyn
    2 Monroe. She was born in Los Angeles on June 1, 1926. As a child, Monroe spent
    3 most of her life in foster homes and an orphanage. At sixteen, she married for the
    4 first time but divorced soon after. It was then that she changed her name to Mari-
    5 lyn Monroe. During World War II, she worked in a factory where she met a photog-
    6 rapher who took photos of her. Hollywood noticed and she soon had small movie
    7 roles that led to larger roles in comedies and dramas. By 1953, Monroe, famous
    8 for playing "dumb blondes," was starring in such movies as Niagara, Gentlemen

9
10
11
12
13

Prefer Blondes, and Billy Wilder's Some Like it Hot. Monroe, the most popular sex symbol of the 1950's, married the baseball player Joe DiMaggio, then the playwright Arthur Miller. Both marriages ended in divorce. Marilyn Monroe died on August 5, 1962 at the age of 36 having battled depression, addiction, and anxiety all her life. Her last film was The Misfits (1961).

CC: Norma Jeane Baker vs. the movie star Marilyn Monroe; baseball player Joe DiMaggio vs. playwright Arthur Miller;
narration: born in Los Angeles on June 1, 1926...as a child...at sixteen...during World War II...met a photographer... small movie roles that led to larger roles... by 1953...married Joe DiMaggio and Arthur Miller; died on August 5, 1962;
description: movie star; foster homes; small movie roles; larger roles; comedies and dramas; battled depression, addiction, and anxiety all her life; the most popular sex symbol of the 1950's; last film;
illustration: starring in such movies as *Niagara*, *Gentlemen Prefer Blondes*, and Billy Wilder's *Some Like it Hot...The Misfits*; (director) Billy Wilder;
CE: both marriages ended in divorce; battled depression, addiction, and anxiety.

Pg. 22   Exercise #5: Listening for Rhetorical Strategies → Audio Track #1

Task: Identify the rhetorical strategies in each sample.

1. There are four red books on the big wooden table in the old white house.

    illustration: books; table; house;
    description: four red books; big wooden table; old white house;

2. Phillip studies harder than Andrew but not as hard as Sylvia, who always get A's.

    illustration: Phillip, Andrew, Sylvia;
    description: Sylvia...always get A's; Phillip studies harder;
    CC: Phillip studies harder than Andrew but not as hard as Sylvia;
    CE: Sylvia (who studies the most) always get A's.

3. Last night it was really raining. Now it is snowing while yesterday it was foggy.

    illustration: last night;
    description: Last night it was really raining. Now it is snowing while yesterday it was foggy.
    CC: last night vs. now vs. yesterday; rain vs. snow vs. fog.

4. Louise is very happy. She got a high TOEFL score because she took a TOEFL class with a great teacher.

    illustration: Louise (example of a successful TOEFL student);
    description: Louise is very happy; a high TOEFL score; a TOEFL class; a great teacher;
    CE: she got a high TOEFL score because she took a TOEFL class with a great teacher.

5. If you eat a lot of fast food, such as French fries, you will become fat, like Peter's brother.

   illustration: French fries; Peter's brother;
   description: fast food; French fries; fat...like Peter's brother;
   CE: if you eat a lot of fast food, such as French fries, you will become fat.

6. Sweden and Norway are big countries; however, Iceland, an island in the North Atlantic Ocean with a population of 340,000 people, is not.

   illustration: Sweden; Norway; Iceland;
   description: Sweden and Norway are big countries; an island in the North Atlantic; a population of 340,000;
   CC: Sweden and Norway vs. Iceland.

7. Michelle doesn't want to talk to Carl. Whenever she did, she thought he was boring, whereas David always has something fascinating to say.

   illustration: Michelle, Carl, David;
   description: Michelle doesn't want to talk to Carl; Carl is boring; David is fascinating;
   CC: Carl boring vs. David fascinating;
   CE: talking to Carl was boring; talking to David is fascinating.

8. Every day, you can see big cars, middle-sized cars, and compact cars.

   illustration: big, middle-sized, and compact cars;
   description: every day; big cars, middle-sized cars, compact cars;
   CC: big cars vs. middle-sized cars vs. compact cars.

9. Veronica prefers tea with milk while Julie prefers coffee with sugar and no milk.

   illustration: Veronica; Julie; tea and coffee;
   description: tea with milk; coffee with sugar and no milk;
   CC: Veronica prefers tea with milk while Julie prefers coffee with sugar and no milk;

10. Because of the train accident, Sarah, an office worker, was late for work. To get to work, she had to take a bus, then take the subway, then walk.

    illustration: Sarah; train accident;
    description: train accident; Sarah, an office worker; late for work;
    CC: bus vs. subway vs walk;
    CE: because of the train accident, Sarah...was late for work;
    process: To get to work, she had to take a bus, then take the subway, then walk.

11. Some students, like Ralph, sit at the back of the class, while some, like Dave, sit on the side and Susan sit at the front. Usually, the smart ones sit at the front of the class, but this is not always true. For example, Patti, an A-student, sits at the back.

illustration: Ralph; Dave; Susan; Patti;
description: some students; sit at the back of the class; sit on the side; sit at the front (of the class); smart ones; an A-student;
CC: sit at the back of the class vs. the side vs. the front; Ralph vs. Dave vs. Susan vs. Patti; Usually, the smart ones sit at the front of the class, but this is not always true.

12. Owls are amazing birds. They have excellent eyesight and exceptional hearing, both of which they use to hunt, typically at night, which makes owls nocturnal.

> **illustration:** owls;
> **description:** owls are amazing birds; excellent eyesight; exceptional hearing; owls (are) nocturnal;
> **CE:** excellent eyesight and exceptional hearing...makes owls nocturnal.

13. Culturally, America and Canada are quite similar; however, politically they are quite dissimilar, especially when it comes to public healthcare.

> **illustration:** America and Canada; public healthcare;
> **description:** culturally; quite similar; public healthcare;
> **CC:** America and Canada culturally similar vs. politically dissimilar.

14. Bibliophobia is a fear of books, whereas suriphobia is a fear of mice.

> **illustration:** bibliophobia; suriphobia;
> **description:** bibliophobia is a fear of books; suriphobia is a fear of mice;
> **CC:** bibliophobia vs. suriphobia.

15. When Americans think of a farm, we typically imagine a house and a red barn with fields full of corn and cows grazing here and there. This type of farm is called a mixed or family farm. A family farm provides income for the family while putting food on their table. This was the most common type of farm up to, and just after, World War Two. In the late 1950's and early 1960's, commercial farms were supplanting the family farm. A commercial farm specializes in growing only one crop, called a cash crop, such as corn or soybeans. Often a corporation will control many commercial farms and produce fruits and vegetables on a massive scale. Some farms specialize in raising livestock for market. Chicken farms and cattle farms fall into this category of farm. Fish farms are also common and supply much of the fresh fish in today's restaurants. With the growth of industrial farming, and the demand for fresh organic produce, many are returning to the family farm as an alternative to mass produced industrial food products. These days, people are eating healthier. As a result, they want to know where their food is coming from.

> **illustration:** family farm; chicken farms; cattle ranches; fish farms;
> **description:** a red barn; fields full of corn; cows grazing here and there; a mixed or family farm; the most common type of farm; in the late 1950's and early 1960's; commercial farms; cash crop; a massive scale; raising livestock; chicken farms and cattle ranches; fish farms; fresh fish in today's restaurants; industrial farm-

ing; fresh organic produce; mass produced industrial food products; eating healthier;

CC: family farms vs. fish farms vs. chicken farms vs. cattle ranches vs. commercial farms;

CE: when Americans think of a farm, we typically imagine a house and a red barn with fields full of corn and cows grazing here and there; A family farm provides income for the family while putting food on their table; Often a corporation will control many commercial farms and produce fruits and vegetables on a massive scale; with the growth of industrial farming, and the demand for fresh organic produce, many are returning to the family farm as an alternative to mass produced industrial food products; these days, people are eating healthier. As a result, they want to know where their food is coming from;

narration: this was the most common type of farm up to and just after World War Two. In the late 1950's and early 1960's, commercial farms were supplanting the family farm.

Pg. 23   Exercise #6: Reasons → Level #1

Task: Identify the cause-and-*effect* reasoning in each. Remember: A reason answers the question why.

1. *Joey failed the test* because he never went to class.

2. The plant didn't get enough sun and water, *so it died.*

3. Use examples *to make an argument more persuasive.*

4. *Susan cried* when her pet dog Leo died.

5. *The band cancelled the show* because it didn't sell any tickets.

6. *Steve was late for work* because he forgot to set his alarm clock.

7. *The students' grades improved* because the teacher gave them extra homework.

8. The company is moving to a smaller city *to save money.*

9. *Lily decided to buy a new computer* when her old computer crashed.

10. *Blame our poor sales* on the economy slowing down.

11. *The drought in California* is due to a lack of rain.

12. Cigarettes *cause cancer and myriad other life-threatening diseases.*

13. Tom's argument *failed to persuade his parents.*

14. The heavy rain *flooded many rivers.*

15. Many people get married *because they want to raise a family.*

Pg. 25   Exercise #7: Reasons → Level #2

Task: Identify the <u>cause</u>-and-*effect* reasoning in each. <u>Remember</u>: A reason answers the question why.

1. <u>If provoked</u>, *a wild animal, such as a bear or a wolf, will attack.*

2. <u>Without a life-support system</u>, *man can't survive in space.*

3. <u>Adding fertilizer to crops</u> *will substantially increase the per-acre yield.*

4. Long ago, <u>a comet streaking across the night sky</u> *caused great consternation among the populace, as comets were harbingers of misfortune.*

5. <u>Stress</u> *is robbing Stan of sleep and the ability to focus at work.*

6. <u>An asteroid struck Earth millions of years ago</u> *and wiped out the dinosaurs.*

7. <u>Properly inflated tires</u> *will ensure better gas mileage and safety.*

8. *To avoid contracting malaria,* <u>take malaria pills when visiting high-risk zones.</u>

9. *Consumers will protest* <u>if the government imposes a tariff on imported products, like smartphones and computers.</u>

10. <u>Practice charity</u>, *for it is a gift that will change your life.*

11. <u>The aroma of the voodoo lily smells like rotting flesh</u> *to attract pollinating flies.*

12. <u>The company should hire more accountants</u> *to improve its record keeping.*

13. *The sky is blue* <u>because molecules in the air scatter blue light more than red.</u>

14. The Shrike is nicknamed "the butcher bird" because <u>after it catches a meal, such as a mouse, it impales it on a branch or thorn</u> *for easier consumption.*

15. <u>Bullying</u> *is a growing social problem that can have life-long effects on a child's self-esteem.*

Pg. 26   Exercise #8: Reasons → Level 3

Task: Identify examples of <u>cause</u>-and-*effect* reasoning in each passage. <u>Remember</u>: A reason answers the question why.

1. 1. An avalanche, also called a snow slide or snow slip, is a great accumulation of
    2. snow and ice that travels rapidly down a mountainside. <u>Most avalanches occur</u>
    3. *without warning.* Why do they start? <u>First, there is so much snow</u> *that gravity*
    4. *pulls it down thus causing a chain reaction in which the weight of the falling*
    5. *snow starts to push other snow downhill.* The second cause is metamorphic.

6   Rocks are heated by the sun *causing ice and snow to melt.* The melting causes
7   *great sheets of snow to move resulting in an avalanche.* Other causes are rain,
8   earthquakes, and rock fall. *To form,* an avalanche needs a slope *with an angle*
9   *shallow enough to hold snow yet steep enough to accelerate the snow once it*
10   *starts moving.* Ninety-percent of avalanches are caused by skiers or snow-
11   boarders in an avalanche zone. They break up the snowpack *which starts the*
12   *snow moving downhill.* Once the avalanche stops, *the snow sets like concrete.*
13   *Bodily movement is next to impossible.* If dug out within fifteen minutes, *you*
14   *will survive. After two hours, very few survive.* If caught in an avalanche, *try*
15   *and get off the slab, the snowpack that is moving. Skiers and snowboards*
16   *should go straight downhill to try and outrace the snow. If you can't escape,*
17   hold on to a tree if possible. Or swim hard. *The human body is heavy and will*
18   *sink.* Once the slide stops, create a breathing space, then punch a hand up to
19   signal your location.

1   2.   On June 18, 1815, *the Napoleonic Era in Europe ended* with Napoleon Bona-
2   parte's defeat at the Battle of Waterloo. Historians argue that Napoleon, one of
3   the greatest military minds in history, *was defeated* for myriad reasons. First,
4   Napoleon, with 73,000 troops, waited too long to attack the Duke of Wellington
5   with 68,000 men. Napoleon, history records, wanted to let the rain-soaked
6   ground dry out first, *but in delaying, he gave time for Prussian General Blucher*
7   *to bring forward his 50,000 strong army. By noon, the time Napoleon ordered the*
8   *attack, he was facing a combined British-Prussian army of over 118,000.* Next,
9   Napoleon took the offensive. He rolled wave after wave of his elite French forces
10   against Wellington's stalwart defenses *and eventually paid the price.* Another
11   reason why Napoleon was defeated at Waterloo is more prosaic: hemorrhoids.
12   Hemorrhoids are an inflation of blood vessels *that prevent the afflicted from sit-*
13   *ting down.* Historians argue that a painful bout of hemorrhoids *prevented Napo-*
14   *leon from riding his horse that day.* As a result, he could not survey the battle-
15   field *thus he was fighting blind.* Whether this is true or not we may never know.
16   Yet this is known. After the battle, 41,000 dead remained on the field. Soon
17   they were beset by locals hunting for teeth, which they extracted and sold to
18   dentists, for false teeth were in high demand. These false teeth became known
19   as Waterloo teeth, and were still being sold in 1860, forty-five years after Water-
20   loo, a battle that changed history.

Pg. 28   Exercise #10: Listening for Reasons → Audio Track #2

Task: Identify examples of cause-and-effect reasoning in each passage. Remember: A reason answers the questions why.

1. Karen worked hard. *As a result, she finished the project on time.*

2. Since Karl started running, *he has been sleeping much better.*

3. The warm spring sun *melted the snow.*

4. Because we have had a lot of snow, *the driving has been extremely dangerous.*

5. *The bread has no taste* <u>because Jill forgot to add salt when she was making it</u>.

6. *Al does not get flu shots* <u>because every time he did</u>, *he always got the flu.*

7. <u>Because of the accident</u>, *Manuel was two hours late getting to work.*

8. *Andy gets terrible headaches* <u>if he uses his computer for more than an hour.</u>

9. <u>If you study and work hard</u>, *your dreams will come true.*

10. <u>A pet</u> *will change your life forever.*

11. <u>An apple a day</u> *keeps the doctor away.*

12. <u>Failure is a good thing</u> *because it teaches you to become stronger and more determined.*

13. <u>Because of the high levels of 0^2</u>, *the government issued an air pollution warning.*

14. <u>Three students were caught cheating on the test</u> *and were permanently expelled.*

15. *Mitch always buys lottery tickets* <u>because he believes that one day he will win.</u>

16. *Samsung recalled the Galaxy Note 7 smartphone* <u>because it had a tendency to explode when charging.</u>

17. <u>After seeing the movie *Jurassic Park*</u>, *Mary was afraid to go outside at night.*

18. *Tom believes that Team USA will win the next World Cup* <u>if it gets a new coach.</u>

19. *Earthquakes are now quite common in Oklahoma,* <u>not because of natural reasons, but because of fracking, a dangerous form of oil extraction</u> *that damages the environment.*

20. <u>During a thunderstorm, if you stand under a tall, pointy object, such as a tree or an umbrella,</u> *you risk being struck by lightning.*

Pg. 30   Exercise #11: Inferring → Level #1

<u>Task</u>: What can you infer from the following? Your inferences may vary.

1. The shoes Allen buys online never fit.

    1. Allen never buys shoes on the internet.
    2. Allen prefers to buy shoes at a store.
    3. Allen buys his clothes from stores.
    4. Allen does most of his shopping on the internet.
    5. Allen trusts the internet to keep his personal information secure.

2. Eva is always late for work.

   1. Eva never sets her alarm.
   2. Eva doesn't like her job.
   3. Eva always gets stuck in traffic.
   4. Eva will soon quit her job.
   5. Eva is lazy.
   6. Eva is distracted by other issues and events in her life.
   7. Working is not a priority for Eva.

3. Anna got a perfect TOEFL score.

   1. Anna studied hard.
   2. Anna was test-ready.
   3. Ann is very happy.
   4. Anna can go to the school of her choosing.
   5. Anna's friends will ask her for TOEFL help.
   6. Anna is a nerd.
   7. Anna has taken the test many times, so she knew what to do to score high.
   8. Anna had a good TOEFL teacher.

4. Beth doesn't use anti-virus software.

   1. Beth thinks anti-virus doesn't work.
   2. Beth doesn't know she needs anti-virus.
   3. Beth has a Mac.
   4. Beth doesn't have a personal computer.
   5. Beth can't afford anti-virus software.

5. Joey has been married five times.

   1. Joey is not the marrying kind.
   2. Joey is still looking for the right wife.
   3. Joey's previous wives broke his heart, so he divorced them all.
   4. Joey cheated on all his wives, so they left him.
   5. Joey is a rich man.
   6. Joey is a poor man owing to legal fees and alimony.
   7. Joey is an alcoholic.

6. Jim sneezes whenever a cat is near.

   1. Jim is allergic to cats.
   2. Jim takes allergy medicine.
   3. Jim does not have a cat.
   4. Jim does not have pets.

7. Erika claims she has seen many ghosts.

   1. Ghosts like Erika.
   2. Erika is a liar.

3. Erika needs attention from friends and family, so she makes up stories like she has seen ghosts.

4. Erika has found a special place with many friendly ghosts.

5. Ghosts are lonely.

6. Ghosts are innocuous.

7. Ghosts do exist, which suggests an after-life of some description.

8. Bridget got another speeding ticket.

1. Bridget always drives fast.

2. Bridget is a dangerous driver.

3. Bridget is impetuous.

4. The police will eventually take Bridget's license away.

5. Bridget could die from speeding.

9. Harvard and Yale accept only the top students in the world.

1. It is hard to get into Yale and Harvard.

2. Harvard and Yale are very selective.

4. Harvard and Yale are competing for the best students in the world.

5. You would be able to get a good job if you graduated from Harvard or Yale.

6. You should apply at other schools not just Harvard and Yale.

7. Bill and Hillary Clinton and George W. Bush were top students.

8. You need a very high TOEFL score when applying to Harvard and Yale.

10. Betty never answers Bobby's emails.

1. Betty is too busy to write Bobby.

2. Betty is not interested in Bobby.

3. Betty has changed her email address and has not told Bobby about it.

4. Betty is telling Bobby to "Go away!"

5. Betty is testing Bobby's love and determination to date her.

6. Betty has found a new love interest.

11. Ali fell asleep in class.

1. Ali was up all last night studying and/or working.

2. Ali thinks the class is boring.

3. Ali has narcolepsy.

4. Ali does not need the credit, so failing is no concern.

12. Jana got a raise at work.

1. Jana asked for a raise and got one.

2. Jana is a hard worker and deserved a raise.

3. Jana is very happy.

4. Jana is not a hard worker. Instead, it was time for a raise for all at work.

5. Jana will celebrate by going shopping.

13. Allen never tells the truth.

  1. Allen can't be trusted.
  2. Allen wants attention, so he lies to get it.
  3. Allen wants to seem more important than he is.
  4. Allen is insecure.
  5. Allen has few friends.

14. Katya can't swim.

  1. Katya is afraid of water.
  2. Katya had a bad experience with water when she was young.
  3. Katya has never taken swimming lessons.
  4. Katya does not have a pool.
  5. Katya does not do water sports, such as surfing or kayaking.
  6. Katya does not own a swimming suit.

15. George told his students they could go home early.

  1. George was finished teaching.
  2. George was sick and needed to end class early to go home.
  3. George had an appointment and had to leave class early.
  4. The students had done well, so George rewarded them with early dismissal.
  5. The students were bad and George just wanted to get rid of them.

Pg. 32   Exercise #12: Inferring → Level #2

<u>Task</u>: What can you infer from the following? Your inferences may vary.

1. Many aquariums have tried to keep a great white shark but each attempt has ended in failure, the great white dying soon after it was displayed.

  1. Great white sharks do not do well in captivity.
  2. Great white sharks should not be kept in aquariums.
  3. A great white shark would attract many people to an aquarium.
  4. Other great white sharks have died in aquariums.
  5. It was a failed experiment.
  6. Aquariums will not be able to display great white sharks.

2. Otzi the Iceman, the 5,000-year-old body found alone and frozen in ice in the Austrian Alps, had an arrow in his back.

  1. Otzi was murdered by friends or strangers.
  2. Otzi was ambushed from behind.
  3. Otzi was carrying something valuable, something his killer wanted.
  4. Otzi had enemies.
  5. Bandits inhabited the Austrian Alps 5,000 years ago.
  6. The path Otzi followed through the alps was not safe.
  7. Otzi's body was well preserved in ice for 5,000 years.

8. Otzi was a great scientific discovery.
9. Otzi was not killed outright. Instead, he died slowly of the arrow wound.

3. Mount Everest is the highest mountain on Earth. To date, more than 250 people have died trying to climb it.

    1. Mt. Everest is very dangerous.
    2. Expect to die if you attempt to climb Mt. Everest.
    3. Those who died were willing to accept the risk.
    4. Despite the dangers, Mt. Everest remains a popular climbing challenge.
    5. Even the best mountain climbers can die on Mt. Everest.

4. When Microsoft introduced its new Windows operating software in 1995, many thought it looked exactly like Apple's operating system.

    1. MS had copied/stolen the Windows idea from Apple.
    2. Apple was mad at MS for copying/stealing the Windows idea.
    3. MS needed a new idea to compete with Apple, so MS "borrowed" Windows.
    4. Apple considered taking to MS to court for copyright/patent infringement.
    5. Bill Gates knew that Windows would make MS a lot of money.
    7. Microsoft shareholders were happy MS was changing to Windows.

5. Donald Trump accused President Barack Obama of not being born in America thus was not eligible to be president; however, Trump never produced any evidence to support his claim, even after five years.

    1. Trump is a racist.
    2. Trump is a liar.
    3. Trump is unpatriotic.
    4. Trump is a sociopath.
    5. Trump is only concerned about Trump.
    6. Trump hates Obama.
    7. Trump found no evidence to support his claim because there was none.
    8. Trump would readily make the same charge against anyone.
    9. Trump is a dangerous man who should not be trusted.

6. On July 2, 1937, Emily Earhart was attempting to be the first women to fly around the world when her plane disappeared over the Pacific Ocean. Years later, in 2012, the heel of her shoe was found on remote Nikumaroro Island.

    1. Earhart's plane ran out of gas and/or had mechanical problems; as a result, it crashed and she survived on Nikumaroro Island.
    2. Earhart sent a radio distress signal that was not received.
    3. Earhart was the only person on the island; there were no natives, villages, etc.
    4. In 1937, flying around the world was perilous since there was no GPS, etc.
    5. People have been searching for Earhart since she crashed.
    6. The heel of Earhart's shoe was made of rubber, a material that lasts a long time.
    7. Earhart knew the risks of flying around the world and accepted them.
    8. The reason for her disappearance has caused much speculation, then and now.

7. Hachiko was a dog who waited for his master every day in front Shibuya Station in Tokyo. When his master died in 1925, Hachiko continued to wait. Hachiko died still waiting in 1935.

   1. Hachiko was very faithful.
   2. Hachiko loved his master.
   3. Hachiko was a dog of resolute character.
   4. Hachiko is a symbol of faith, love, and resolve for the people of Japan.

8. When the stock market crashed in 1929, many on Wall Street jumped out of windows to their deaths.

   1. Many were suddenly bankrupt and had nothing left to live for, so they jumped.
   2. Many were stockbrokers; they had lost other peoples' investment money and, full of shame and guilt, they committed suicide.

9. To this day, some Americans say that the American Civil War was fought to free the slaves while others say it was fought to defend states' rights.

   1. The American Civil War is still being fought to this day.
   2. The reasons for the Civil War divide Americans, then and now.
   3. Your opinion about the Civil War depends on which side you were on: the South, which was pro-slavery, or the North, which was anti-slavery.

10. In America, the thumbs-up sign means "Okay!" or "Good!" while in other countries, this same sign has a pejorative meaning.

    1. Not all hand signs have the same meaning.
    2. Symbolic meaning is culture-specific.
    3. An American could easily insult a non-American by using what he/she thinks is a positive hand sign in a country other than America.

11. Warren Buffet, the richest man in America, eats junk food every day. He has a particular fondness for Cheetos and Coke.

    1. Mr. Buffet is neither a vegan nor a vegetarian.
    2. Mr. Buffet is not concerned about his diet or his health.
    3. Mr. Buffet is really just a simple man who likes simple food.
    4. There is no connection between wealth and taste.
    5. Despite his wealth and intelligence, Mr. Buffet is not a symbol of healthy living.
    6. Mr. Buffet's staff eats junk food to be like their boss.
    7. Mr. Buffet would probably invite you out for a hamburger.

12. When Annie and Lily went for a walk in the forest, they saw a deer with two fawns.

    1. The mother deer had twins.
    2. One of the fawns lost its mother and was adopted by the mother deer.

13. Scientists refuse to investigate, or even consider, evidence of UFOs.

   1. *Scientists do not believe that UFOs (unidentified flying objects) exist.*
   2. *Scientists will reject any non-scientific evidence attempting to prove the existence of UFOs.*
   3. *The government also rejects the idea of UFOs.*
   4. *If you see a UFO, do not report it to a scientist. You will not be believed.*
   5. *If scientists reject the existence of UFOs, then they reject the idea of bigfoot, the Loch Ness monster, Ogopogo, and many other unexplained phenomena.*

14. It takes one gallon of water to grow one almond and five gallons for one walnut.

   1. *Farmers who grow almonds and walnuts have high water bills.*
   2. *Consumers pay a lot of money for almonds and walnuts.*
   3. *Growing almonds and walnuts is contributing to the water shortage problem in California, where they are mainly grown.*
   4. *Farms that grow almonds and walnuts have complex irrigation systems.*
   5. *Farms must be near available and constant water sources.*

15. The average internet user spends less than 20 seconds on a web site before clicking over to another site. The result is the mind has little or no time to concentrate. This, doctor says, reduces the brain's ability to retain information in the long-term memory part of the brain.

   1. *People get bored quickly surfing the web.*
   2. *People enjoy clicking from site to site; it is like an addiction.*
   3. *Clicking from site to site is not good for concentration or long-term memory.*
   4. *Surfing the internet is unhealthy.*
   5. *To develop your long-term memory, turn off the internet and read a book.*

Pg. 34   Exercise #13: Inferring → Level #3

Task: What can you infer from the following? Your inferences may vary.

1. William Shakespeare is considered the greatest writer in the English language. He was born in born Stratford in April 1563, the exact date not known. In 1582, when he was eighteen, he married Anne Hathaway. They had three children. Around 1588, Shakespeare moved his family to London where he went on to write 38 plays, including *Hamlet, Romeo and Juliet,* and *Othello.* Yet in 1598, the Stratford town record describes resident William Shakespeare as a grain hoarder and a tax dodger. When he died in 1616, his death went unnoticed while lesser writers were given elaborate funerals attended by royalty. Moreover, the poetry on his headstone is of inferior quality. In his will, he made no mention of his plays or poems or manuscripts, or how to dispose of them. Indeed, there is no evidence that Shakespeare ever wrote a letter or that he was even literate. Six signatures are the only lasting evidence; three are incomplete while the other three are barely legible. His wife was illiterate as were those around him. All this stands in stark contrast to the London playwright whose plays reference a world of knowledge, including Greek philosophy and tragedy, and moreover, political intrigue. He knew naval and military strategy and had an intimate knowledge of royal pastimes, including

17　the art of falconry. The original Shakespeare monument in Stratford did not show
18　a writer holding a quill or a book. Instead, it showed a man holding a bag grain,
19　indicating that he was a grain merchant. Some argue that the real William Shake-
20　speare was Edward de Vere, Earl of Oxford, and that for political and social rea-
21　sons, he had to conceal his identity. De Vere was a noted patron of the arts, poet
22　and playwright. His erratic and volatile behavior (he impregnated one of Elizabeth
23　1's maids of honor) got him exiled from court, yet he returned to favor and went
24　on to become Elizabeth's "the most excellent of Elizabeth's courtier poets."

1　*Line 3: Shakespeare married young. Maybe he wanted to get away from his par-*
2　*ents. Maybe his love for Anne Hathaway was not true love but blind love.*
3　*Line 4-5: Maybe Shakespeare felt there were more opportunities for writing plays in*
4　*London, so he moved there.*
5　*Lines 5-14: The Shakespeare on record in Stratford was a criminal. He was not fa-*
6　*mous or rich. It seems he was not a writer either. His illegible signature suggests he*
7　*could not even write. This suggests he was illiterate. If so, how could he write plays?*
8　*Lines 13-17: The Shakespeare on record in London was well-educated and close to*
9　*power, information he used in his plays.*
10　*Lines 17-25: The statue in Stratford suggests that Shakespeare was not a writer but*
11　*a merchant instead. This suggests that the real Shakespeare was somebody else,*
12　*someone unknown, like the Earl of Oxford, as the passage suggests. This passage*
13　*suggests that the true Shakespeare will never be known.*

1　2.　Light travels at 186,282 miles per second or 299,792 kilometers. A light-year is
2　the distance light travels in one year. That distance is 6 trillion miles or 9 tril-
3　lion kilometers. The observable universe, that which is known to mankind, is a
4　staggering 92 billion light-years in diameter. Within that space are billions of
5　galaxies, stars, and planets. Our galaxy, the Milky Way, is 100,000 light-years
6　in diameter. It contains approximately 400 billion star systems like our sun
7　and its planets. How many galaxies are there? One scientist said, "There are
8　more galaxies in the universe than there are grains of sand on all the beaches
9　of Earth." As you can see, the universe is huge, so much so that it is hard to
10　imagine just how big. And that is only the known universe. But all this raises
11　an interesting question: Are we humans on planet Earth the only life form in
12　the universe?

1. Distances and speeds in space are beyond human imagining.
2. Because the universe is so vast, the chance of life existing elsewhere is likely.
3. We know very little about the universe.

Pg. 35　Exercise #14: Writing and Inferring

Task: Write sentences in which your reader must infer your meaning. Your inferences may vary. Below are sample sentences and sample inferences.

1.　ice cream

sample: *Fred ate all the ice cream - again!*

<u>What can we infer about Fred and ice cream?</u>

1. Fred loves ice cream.
2. Fred has a sweet tooth.
3. Fred is selfish.
4. Fred was hungry.
5. Fred is predictable.

2. money

    <u>sample</u>: *Sylvia found a wallet full of <u>money</u> in the park last Sunday.*

    <u>What can we infer Sylvia and the wallet she found?</u>

    1. Sylvia was surprised when she found the wallet.
    2. Sylvia tried to return the wallet and the money.
    3. Sylvia kept the money because she needed it.
    4. Sylvia likes to walk in the park on Sundays.

3. reef

    <u>sample</u>: *Coral on the Great Barrier <u>Reef</u> in Australia is dying at an alarming rate.*

    <u>What can we infer about coral and the Great Barrier Reef?</u>

    1. Global warming is killing the Great Barrier Reef in Australia.
    2. If the Great Barrier Reef in Australia disappears, other species will too.
    3. If the Great Barrier Reef disappears, tourism will be impacted.
    4. If Great Barrier Reef is dying, other reefs are also dying.
    5. If other reefs are dying, myriad other ocean species are also dying.
    6. The death of the Great Barrier Reef and other reefs will result in a catastrophic change in the world's oceans, one that will directly affect mankind.

4. married

    <u>sample</u>: *Dave and Tina got divorced soon after they got <u>married</u>.*

    <u>What can we infer Dave and Tina?</u>

    1. Dave and Tina were not made for each other.
    2. Dave and Tina did not marry for love.
    3. Dave and Tina quickly came to their decision to divorce.
    4. Something serious caused Dave and Tina to reach their decision so quickly.
    5. Dave and Tina were too young to get married, and they realized it.
    6. Dave's and/or Tina's parents are also divorced/separated.
    7. Dave and Tina had no children.
    8. Dave and Tina had a child, which is why they got married.

5. dictionary

sample: Ann uses a _dictionary_ when she studies Spanish.

What can we infer Ann and dictionaries?
1. Ann is learning how to speak Spanish.
2. Ann likes to look up the meaning of Spanish words.
3. Ann is making a Spanish word list.
4. Ann is taking Spanish classes.
5. Ann is planning a trip to a Spanish-speaking country.

6. solution

sample: John asked Sue to help him find a _solution_ to his problem.

What can we infer John and Sue?

1. John trusts Sue.
2. John has tried but has been unsuccessful finding a solution.
3. Sue is good at solving problems.
4. Sue is a coworker/friend.
5. Sue has helped John with prior problems.

7. sick

sample: Max has been _sick_ in bed at home for a month.

What can we infer Max?

1. Max is very sick.
2. Max has missed a lot of school or work, or both.
3. Many are worried about Max's health.
4. The illness is serious.
5. Max is taking a lot of medication.

8. bank

sample: The _bank_ on the corner closed permanently last month and is now a Macdonald's.

What can we infer about the bank?

1. The bank was not making new customers, so it closed.
2. The bank was losing money, so it closed.
3. The bank was not in a good location for banking customers.
4. The location is a better place for a fast food restaurant.

9. airplane

   sample: *The passenger <u>airplane</u> was forced to land at a different airport.*

   <u>What can we infer the airplane</u>?

   1. An emergency forced the plane to change directions.
   2. The passengers will not reach their destinations on time.
   3. When the plane landed, security converged on the plane.
   4. The plane had a mechanical problem.
   5. The weather was bad at the airport where the plane was supposed to land.

10. bake

    sample: *Adam <u>baked</u> a cake without a recipe, and it was a disaster.*

    <u>What can we infer Adam and baking</u>?

    1. Adam will use a recipe the next time he bakes a cake.
    2. Adam does not like using directions.
    3. Adam will learn from his mistake and ask for advice next time.
    4. Adam threw the cake out.
    5. Adam's friends said his cake was, "Great!"

11. lion

    sample: *The <u>lion</u> watched as the zebras approached.*

    <u>What can we infer the lion and the zebras</u>?

    1. The lion is hungry.
    2. The lion is stalking the zebras.
    3. There are probably other lions about since lions live and hunt in prides.
    4. The zebras are unaware of the lion/lions stalking them.
    5. The lion/lions will attack when the zebras are close enough.

12. diet

    sample: *This is the third <u>diet</u> Helga has tried this month.*

    <u>What can we infer about Helga and dieting</u>?

    1. Helga is searching for the right diet.
    2. Helga is not happy with the diets she has tried.
    3. Helga has no discipline when it comes to staying on a diet.
    4. Helga likes to try new things, like diets.
    5. Helga is not serious about dieting.

13. work

sample: *Mike does not mind staying late at <u>work</u>.*

<u>What can we infer about Mike and work</u>?

1. Mike likes his job.
2. Mike gets paid overtime.
3. Mike wants to make a good impression to get a raise or a promotion.
4. Mike lives close to work.

14. accident

sample: *The witness who saw the <u>accident</u> has vanished.*

<u>What can we infer about the accident and the witness</u>?

1. The witness does not want to become involved with the accident.
2. The witness does not want to talk to the police.
3. The witness is the victim of foul play.
4. The witness thinks the accident was not that serious, so there was no point in getting involved.
5. The witness will eventually show up and report what he/she saw.

15. music

sample: *Melissa can't sleep at night because her neighbor's <u>music</u> is too loud.*

<u>What can we infer about Melissa and her neighbor's music</u>?

1. Melissa is losing sleep and getting stressed out.
2. Melissa will ask the neighbor to turn the music down at night.
3. Melissa will complain to her landlord/police.
4. Melissa will move.
5. Melissa will buy earplugs.

Pg. 36   <u>Exercise #15</u>: Listening and Inferring → Audio Track #3

<u>Task</u>: What is each sample inferring? Your inferences will vary.

1. Lucy is going shopping tomorrow for a new dress and a new pair of shoes.

<u>What can we infer about Lucy</u>?

1. Lucy has a job interview.
2. Lucy has a date.
3. Lucy feels like buying some new clothes.
4. Lucy is going to a party.

2. Lucas is starving.

    <u>What can we infer about Lucas?</u>

    1. Lucas is really hungry.
    2. Lucas hasn't eaten in a long time.
    3. Lucas wants to eat.

3. Bob believes that a house is a wise investment.

    <u>What can we infer about Bob?</u>

    1. Bob will buy a house.
    2. Bob will tell his friends they should save their money and buy a house.
    3. Bob prefers to live in an house rather than an apartment.

4. Betty has three after-school jobs.

    <u>What can we infer about Betty?</u>

    1. Betty is a hard worker.
    2. Betty needs money to pay bills, etc.
    3. Each job is part-time and does not pay that well.
    4. Betty is struggling to make ends meet.
    5. When it is time to study, Betty is exhausted.
    6. Betty is supporting a child while going to school.
    7. Betty is resolute.

5. Carmella goes to the beach every weekend in the summer.

    <u>What can we infer about Carmella?</u>

    1. Carmella loves the beach.
    2. Carmella loves swimming in the ocean/lake.
    3. Carmella enjoys water sports.
    4. Carmella would like to live by the water.
    5. Carmella views the beach as a form of escape from her job, etc.

6. Nancy's cat and dog sleep in the same bed at night.

    <u>What can we infer about Nancy's cat and dog?</u>

    1. Nancy's cat and dog are friends.
    2. Nancy's cat and dog do not fight.
    3. Nancy's cat and dog are spoiled.
    4. Nancy does not let her cat or her dog sleep on her bed at night.

7. Jennifer loses her car keys at least once a week.

   <u>What can we infer about Jennifer?</u>

   1. Jennifer is forgetful.
   2. Jennifer is not very organized.
   3. Jennifer is often late for work or appointments.
   4. Jennifer loses other things as well, like her glasses and her phone, etc.

8. Last night, Greg ordered a large pizza and ate it all. Later, he had a stomachache.

   <u>What can we infer about Greg?</u>

   1. Greg was starving.
   2. Greg loves pizza.
   3. Greg was alone last night.
   4. Greg ate too much.
   5. Greg will not eat so much the next time he orders a pizza.
   6. Greg took medication for his upset stomach.

9. The company rejected the offer made by the government.

   <u>What can we infer about the company?</u>

   1. The company was not impressed by the government's offer/plan.
   2. The company has a better plan.
   3. The company does not want to work with the government.
   4. The company has had a better offer.

10. Bill texts when driving.

    <u>What can we infer about Bill?</u>

    1. Bill is a dangerous driver.
    2. Bill is addicted to his phone.
    3. Bill is going to have an accident and cause serious injury to himself and others.
    4. Bill does not think of other drivers.
    5. Bill does not obey the law; (Texting while driving in the U.S. is illegal).
    6. Bill is putting the passengers in his car at serious risk of death or injury.

11. Joan is against animal cruelty.

    <u>What can we infer about Joan?</u>

    1. Joan is a vegetarian/vegan.
    2. Joan's husband/boyfriend is also a vegetarian/vegan.
    3. Joan does not eat meat.
    4. Joan does not wear leather.
    5. Joan belongs to animal protection groups.
    6. Joan donates money to animal protection groups.

12. Joey is always late paying off his credit cards.

    <u>What can we infer about Joey?</u>

    1. Joey uses his credit cards to pay for everything.
    2. Joey does not save money to pay his bills.
    3. Joey is late paying all his bills, such as his rent/ mortgage, etc.
    4. Joey has a bad credit rating.
    5. Joey can't manage his money.
    6. Joey prefers to spend money not on bills but on himself.
    7. Joey is accumulating a lot of credit card debt.
    8. Joey is a spendthrift.

13. Jonas Salk, the scientist who has saved millions of lives with the invention of the polio vaccine, refused to accept any money for his work.

    <u>What can we infer about Jonas Salk?</u>

    1. Jonas Salk was a genius.
    2. Jonas Salk was not interested in money only in saving lives.
    3. Many owe their lives to Jonas Salk's invention.
    4. If Jonas Salk had accepted money, he would've been very rich.
    5. Jonas Salk changed the course of medicine and medical history.
    6. Jonas Salk won many awards for his achievement.
    7. Jonas Salk felt great pride in his accomplishment.

14. Dinosaurs lived 250 million years ago, whereas humans appeared 200,000 years ago. The Earth itself is four billion years old.

    <u>What can we infer from this passage?</u>

    1. Planet Earth is very old.
    2. Humans are a new species and have evolved little.
    3. Humans have not been on Earth very long.
    4. If dinosaurs can become extinct, so too can other species, like humans.
    5. Life on Earth is continually changing and evolving.

15. Neil Armstrong, the astronaut who first stepped on the Moon, did not enjoy the celebrity of his status and always kept a low profile as he taught engineering at a university.

    <u>What can we infer about Neil Armstrong?</u>

    1. Neil Armstrong was a modest man.
    2. Neil Armstrong did want to be famous or a celebrity.
    3. Neil Armstrong viewed walking on the moon as just doing his job, nothing more.
    4. Neil Armstrong enjoyed teaching.
    5. Neil Armstrong was a very private man who rarely talked to the media.

Pg. 37   Exercise #16: Topic + Controlling Idea → Level #1

Task: Identify the topic (T) and controlling idea (C) in each.

1. David and Susan bought a new house.

   T: David and Susan
   C: bought a new house

2. Traveling is so much fun.

   T: traveling
   C: is so much fun

3. Annie believes that hard work leads to success.

   T: Annie
   C: believes that hard work leads to success

4. Robins are the first birds to return in spring.

   T: robins
   C: are the first birds to return in spring

5. The oldest city in the United States is St. Augustine in Florida.

   T: St. Augustine in Florida
   C: is the oldest city in the United States

6. Contrary to popular belief, cats and dogs are not natural enemies.

   T: cats and dogs
   C: are not natural enemies contrary to popular belief

7. Skiing and snowboarding are two popular winter sports.

   T: skiing and snowboarding
   C: are two popular winter sports

8. After Professor Smith read Brenda's essay, he told her it was excellent.

   T: Professor Smith
   C: he told her (Brenda) it (her essay) was excellent after he talked to her

9. The first great battle of the American Civil War was the battle of Bull Run.

   T: the battle of Bull Run
   C: was the first great battle of the American Civil War

10. A good example of a hard worker is Paul.

    T: Paul
    C: is a good example of a hard worker

11. Professional athletes are paid too much.

    T: professional athletes
    C: are paid too much

12. Being accepted into Harvard was not what Lucy expected.

    T: Lucy
    C: being accepted into Harvard was not what she expected

13. In America, pizza is round whereas in many countries, it is square.

    T: pizza
    C: in America it is round, whereas in many countries, it is square

14. Studying for TOEFL takes time and preparation.

    T: studying for TOEFL
    C: takes time and preparation

15. The process of buying a house can be stressful.

    T: the process of buying a house
    C: can be stressful

16. Making a wish is said to bring luck.

    T: making a wish
    C: is said to bring good luck

Pg. 39   Exercise #17: Topic + Controlling Idea → Level #2

Task: Identify the topic (T) and controlling idea (C) in each.

1. The assassination of archduke Franz Ferdinand in Sarajevo on June 28, 1914 was the spark that ignited the First World War.

    T: the assassination of archduke Franz Ferdinand
    C: was the spark that ignited the First World War

2. Inasmuch as is a synonym for because.

    T: inasmuch as
    C: is a synonym for because

3. Yellow fever is a blood disease transmitted by mosquitoes to humans.

    T: yellow fever
    C: is a blood disease transmitted by mosquitoes to humans

4. If Mary had known that Charles was going to be at the party, she would not have gone.

    T: Mary
    C: she would not have gone to the party if she had known that Charles was going to be there

5. Defined, a polar vortex is a mass of Arctic air that moves south in winter and settles over Canada and the United States, bringing high winds and dangerously low temperatures.

    T: a polar vortex
    C: is a mass of Arctic air that moves south in winter and settles over Canada and the United States

6. Albert Einstein said, "The true sign of intelligence is not knowledge but imagination."

    T: Albert Einstein
    C: said, "The true sign of intelligence is not knowledge but imagination."

7. The Elbe River in Spain is home to world-record catfish.

    T: the Elbe River
    C: is home to world-record catfish

8. George believes that life exists in the universe and that one day we will find it while Federica believes that life does not exist, that humans are the only life form in the universe.

    T: George
    C: believes that life exists in the universe
    T: Federica
    C: believes that life does not exist in the universe.

9. The air pollution is so bad in Beijing, the airport often shuts down inasmuch as planes cannot take off or land due to reduced visibility.

    T: Beijing
    C: the air pollution is so bad, the airport often shuts down

10. Chemistry and biology were the subjects Clarissa enjoyed the most in high school whereas English and French were the subjects she liked the least.

    T: Clarissa
    C: in high school, chemistry and biology were the subjects she enjoyed the most whereas English and French were the subjects she liked the least

11. Cancer, emphysema, and chronic bronchitis are just a few of the crippling diseases you can get from smoking.

    T: cancer, emphysema, and chronic bronchitis
    C: are just a few of the crippling diseases you can get from smoking

12. The professors discussed the issue brought before them by the students and decided that the dean should hear about it and decide for herself what to do.

    T: the professors
    C: discussed the issue brought before them by the students

13. Most countries have one national sport; however, Canada has two. Hockey is Canada's national winter sport while lacrosse is the national summer sport.

    T: Canada
    C: has two national sports: hockey and lacrosse

14. Homo Sapiens is the scientific name for humans.

    T: Homo Sapiens
    C: is the scientific name for humans

15. Sleeplessness, decreased urine output, headaches, and constipation are all signs of dehydration. How can you remedy dehydration? Drink more water.

    T: dehydration
    C: sleeplessness, decreased urine output, headaches, and constipation
       are all signs of dehydration

Pg. 40   Exercise #18: Topic + Controlling Idea → Level #3

Task: Identify the topic (T) and controlling idea (C) in each.

1. U.K. lawyers are called barristers and solicitors, whereas in America, a lawyer is both a barrister and a solicitor.

    T: U.K. lawyers
    C: are called barristers and solicitors
    T: in America
    C: a lawyer is both a barrister and a solicitor

2. Is the Chicxulub Crater under the Yucatan Peninsula in Mexico evidence of the asteroid that struck the Earth and wiped out the dinosaurs? That theory, while indeed compelling, remains controversial.

    T: the Chicxulub Crater
    C: Is it evidence of the asteroid that struck the Earth and wiped out the dinosaurs?

3. A major event in the world of science was Nicolaus Copernicus' formulating of a model of the universe that placed the sun, not the Earth, at the center of our solar system.

    T: a major event in the world of science
    C: was Nicolaus Copernicus' formulating of a model of the universe that placed the sun, not the Earth, at the center of our solar system

4. In order to reach their breeding grounds, wildebeest, or gnus, must overcome many obstacles, including the Mara River, where crocodiles lie in wait.

    T: wildebeest
    C: must overcome many obstacles in order to reach their breeding grounds

5. A complex neuro-physiological process is left-right discrimination. For most, it is second nature; however, many struggle telling their left from their right. Why is that?

    T: a complex neuro-physiological process
    C: is left-right discrimination

6. Leonardo da Vinci is an acknowledged genius, a true Renaissance man who designed myriad revolutionary ideas, such as the first helicopter; however, as a painter, historical records confirm that he disappointed many of his patrons by failing to finish a work on time or not at all. That such few da Vinci paintings exist underscores this fact.

    T: Leonardo da Vinci
    C: a great man who disappointed many of his patrons

7. Socrates (470-399 BC) was a Greek philosopher famous for developing what today is known as the Socratic method, a system of cooperative argumentative dialogue between individuals aimed at stimulating critical thinking through the asking and answering of questions. This dialectal method of discourse between opposing viewpoints remains the cornerstone of the western educational tradition.

    T: Socrates
    C: was a Greek philosopher famous for developing the Socratic method

8. In 1941, a German military officer in Russia filmed a woolly mammoth, an animal that had supposedly been extinct for over 10,000 years. However, it was later proven that the film was indeed a hoax.

   T: a German military officer
   C: supposedly filmed an extinct woolly mammoth

9. They are found on every continent but Antarctica and instill fear in many. They can spin silken webs five times stronger than steel. They have eight legs and blue blood. They can grow as wide as eleven inches and as small as the head of a pin. Some are so deadly one bite will kill you while others make excellent pets. Some are considered living fossils while others can run two feet per second. Some give presents while some can jump forty times their body length. Contrary to popular belief, they are not insects, like flies and ants. Instead, they are arachnids or spiders.

   T: spiders
   C: they are found on every continent but Antarctica and instill fear in many. They can spin silken webs five times stronger than steel. They have eight legs and blue blood. They can grow as wide as eleven inches and as small as the head of a pin. Some are so deadly one bite will kill you while others make excellent pets. Some are considered living fossils while others can run two feet per second. Some give presents while some can jump forty times their body length. Contrary to popular belief, they are not insects, like flies and ants. They are arachnids...or more simply → C: have many unique characteristics

10. Past is prologue.

    T: Past
    C: is prologue

11. There are many firsts in history: the first car, the first radio, the first vaccine. However, few firsts compare to the introduction of the printing press in 1468 by Johannes Gutenberg. Gutenberg, a German blacksmith, created mechanical movable type printing. The result was the Bible could be mass produced. This allowed more people to read and ultimately created the modern, knowledge-based world we know today.

    T: the printing press by Johannes Gutenberg
    C: was a first in history

12. Look up? What do you see? Straight white lines crisscrossing the clear blue sky. Are they clouds? Yes. More specifically, they are jet contrails. Let me explain. Jets fly at extremely high altitudes where it is very cold, as cold as -50 C. The hot exhaust of the jet's engines contains a lot of water. When that water hits the cold ambient air, it condenses and freezes creating ice crystals. Those crystals are jet contrails.

    T: jet contrails
    C: are white lines in the sky left by jets

13. The Harrier, or "jump jet", is a British combat jet capable of vertical takeoff and landing. It gets its name from the species of diurnal hawks called harriers, which form the Circinae sub-family of the Accipitridae family of birds of prey.

    T: the Harrier
    C: is a British combat jet capable of vertical takeoff and landing

14. Visit the cooking oil section in your local grocery store and you will find myriad oils with which to cook and season. Of those oils, olive oil is the healthiest. It is high in the phytonutrient oleocanthal, which mimics the anti-inflammatory effects of ibuprofen. This can aid in cancer prevention and reduce joint pain. Olive oil can also reduce the levels of blood cholesterol, LDL-cholesterol, and triglycerides while not altering the level of HDL-cholesterol.

    T: olive oil
    C: is the healthiest oil

15. Modern political theory owes much to *The Prince*, a book by Niccolo Machiavelli in which Machiavelli describes the ideal leader, a person lacking in morals in order to do whatever it takes to succeed, a man such as Donald Trump.

    T: *The Prince*
    C: a book by Niccolo Machiavelli in which he describes the ideal leader

Pg. 44   Exercise #20: Listening → Topic + Controlling Idea → Audio Track #4

Task: Identify the topic (T) and controlling idea (C) in each.

1. Cynthia can't eat nuts.

    T: Cynthia
    C: can't eat nuts

2. Bill Gates dropped out of Harvard to get into the computer business.

    T: Bill Gates
    C: dropped out of Harvard to get into the computer business

3. The fastest land animal in the world is the cheetah.

    T: the cheetah
    C: the fastest land animal in the world

4. Women in the United States are paid less than men at all levels.

    T: women in the United States
    C: are paid less than men at all levels

5. A tsunami is a dangerous ocean wave caused by an earthquake.

   T: a tsunami
   C: is a dangerous ocean wave caused by an earthquake

6. A wildfire fire is the uncontrolled burning of dry vegetation in the countryside.

   T: a wildfire fire
   C: is the uncontrolled burning of dry vegetation in the countryside

7. Due to a lack of nutrition, children all over the world die every day.

   T: children all over the world
   C: die every day due to a lack of nutrition

8. The bobcat is a wild cat that lives in the forests of North America.

   T: the bobcat
   C: is a wild cat that lives in the forests of North America

9. Deep in the jungles of Central and South America are birds which follow army ants. As the ants move through the jungle, they flush out insects which the birds eat. In this way, these birds, known as ant followers or antbirds, depend on the ants for their survival.

   T: ant followers or antbirds
   C: depend on army ants for their survival

10. According to a United Nations' report, emissions from cattle raising are the world's biggest source of greenhouse gas.

    T: emissions from cattle raising
    C: are the world's biggest source of greenhouse gas

11. In 1938, German archaeologist Wilhelm Konig discovered an earthwaren jar in the National Museum of Iraq in Bagdad. The 2,000 year-old jar was the size of a fist and contained an iron rod surrounded by a copper cylinder. Konig believed that he had stumbled upon the world's first battery, but this notion has since been dispelled.

    T: German archaeologist Wilhelm Konig
    C: he believed he had discovered the world's first battery

12. Even today, there are those who believe that the Earth is not spherical but flat. This group of naysayers is called the Flat Earth Society.

    T: the Flat Earth Society
    C: they believe the Earth is flat

13. Why did the Neanderthals, an early race of humans, suddenly disappear from Europe 40,000 years ago? Conventional wisdoms points at our ancestors, Homo Sapiens. They moved into Europe from Africa and eventually drove the Neanderthals into extinction. However, new research in the journal *Nature* argues that the Italian super volcano, Campi Flegrei, exploded and sent ash clouds all over Europe. As a result, Europe suddenly got colder, an ice age occurred, and the Neanderthals, unable to survive the extreme climatic change, disappeared.

    T: Neanderthals
    C: new research says a super volcano, and not Homo Sapiens, drove them into extinction

14. Few outside the science world know the name Mary Somerville. She was a self-taught genius born in Scotland in 1780. Many regard her as the Queen of nineteenth-century science. It was because of Somerville that the term scientist was created. In 1834, at age 53, Somerville wrote a paper called *On the Connexion of the Physical Sciences*. It was well received; however, the reviewer of the paper did not know how to describe Somerville. He could not call her "a man of science," for she was not a man. But she was indeed a first. Somerville was the first woman to write on math and astronomy. The reviewer of her paper ended up creating a new word for her: scientist. And that is how the word scientist entered the English language.

    T: Mary Somerville
    C: how the word scientist was created to describe her and her achievements

15. Rap and hip hop contain lyrics that are often hard, if not impossible, to understand. That is because the lyrics used are slang. Slang is invented words designed to be shared and be understood by members of a select group or gang, and to keep unwanted people, like the police, out. In this way, slang is a form of exclusionary code.

    T: Rap and hip hop lyrics
    C: are an invented code called slang

Pg. 52   Exercise #21: Rhetorical Strategy Analysis

<u>Task</u>: Identify the rhetorical strategies used to develop the short personal essay.

cause-and-*effect*

1. **We need zoos** <u>*because they are educational*</u>.
2. **By going to the zoo**, <u>*you can definitely learn something new.*</u>

description

when I was twelve...wild animals...real life...really big...Toronto zoo

compare-and-contrast

On TV, (the lions) looked so small, but when I saw them live, they were really big.

Pg. 58   Exercise #24: Thesis Identification → Level 1

1	ST	4	OT	7	ST	10	ST	13	NT
2	NT	5	NT	8	OT	11	OT	14	ST
3	NT	6	NT	9	ST	12	NT	15	NT

Pg. 59   Exercise #25: Thesis Identification → Level 2

1	NT	4	OT	7	ST	10	ST	13	NT
2	OT	5	NT	8	NT	11	NT	14	ST
3	NT	6	ST	9	NT	12	NT	15	NT

Pg. 60   Exercise #26: Thesis Identification → Level 3

1	ST	4	NT	7	OT	10	OT	13	OT
2	OT	5	NT	8	NT	11	OT	14	ST
3	OT	6	OT	9	OT	12	OT	15	OT

Pg. 62   Exercise #27: Listening → Thesis Identification → Audio Track #5

Task: Analyze each statement. If it is a subjective thesis, put ST beside it. If it is an objective thesis, put OT. If it is not a thesis, put NT.

1	People who fear blood are called hemophobics.	OT
2	Moby Dick is the story of a white whale that attacks and sinks a whaling ship.	OT
3	A weed is an invasive plant that thrives in a new environment.	OT
4	Donald got a sunburn because he didn't use any suntan lotion.	NT
5	Personally, I think the project failed due to a lack of investor interest.	ST
6	Killer whales live and hunt in family groups called pods.	OT
7	When Professor Stirling enters the room, everyone falls silent.	NT
8	One question all students ask is, "Will I get a job after I graduate?"	NT
9	Florida: fun and sun!	NT
10	All women have the right to choose the course and destiny of their lives without inference from the government or anyone else.	ST
11	Good morning, class. Today I want to talk about the homework. I realize that the assignment was quite difficult; however, this is the type of material you can expect on the exam, so it's best to practice it now. If you have any questions, I will be in my office today and tomorrow between 3 and 4 p.m.	NT
12	Therapy dogs help children overcome speech and emotional disorders.	OT

13	An idiom is a comparison that can be either direct or indirect.	OT
14	Turmeric is called the goddess of spice for good reason. As an anti-bacterial, it fights infections; as an anti-oxidant, it boosts the immune system; as an anti-inflammatory, it aids in digestion and protects against arthritis.	OT
15	One of the most famous battles of the War of 1812 was the battle for Queenston Heights near Niagara Falls in Canada.	OT

Part II - Academic English Practice

PG.	TASK	?#	ANSWERS	
99	Structure	1	A	
	→ Exercise #1	2	B	
		3	D	
		4	A	
		5	D	
		6	B	
		7	B	
		8	C	
		9	B	
		10	C	
		11	B	
		12	B	
				CORRECTIONS
101	Written Expression	1	C	or
	→ Exercise #1	2	A	first
		3	D	a class
		4	B	took
		5	D	of which
		6	A	with
		7	D	retaking the test
		8	A	~~it~~
		9	D	in
		10	D	success
		11	C	you can ask ETS to
		12	A	On test day
		13	B	times
		14	D	break
		15	C	for
		16	A	resource
		17	A	will test
		18	C	who has/who's
		19	C	on

PG.	TASK	?#	ANSWERS	
101	Written Expression (cont'd)	20	D	the
	→ Exercise #1	21	B	independent
		22	C	to a school
103	Vocabulary	1	A	
	→ Exercise #1	2	A	
		3	A	
		4	C	
		5	D	
		6	C	
		7	D	
		8	C	
		9	A	
		10	A	
		11	A	
		12	A	
		13	B	
		14	D	
		15	A	
		16	A	
		17	D	
		18	A	

PG.	TASK	?#	ANSWERS	
104	Structure	1	A	
	→ Exercise #2	2	D	
		3	B	
		4	C	
		5	B	
		6	A	
		7	D	
		8	B	
		9	D	
		10	A	
		11	B	
		12	A	
				CORRECTIONS
106	Written Expression	1	C	time management
	→ Exercise #2	2	C	while
		3	D	through
		4	B	discussion

PG.	TASK	?#	ANSWERS	CORRECTIONS
106	Written Expression (cont'd)	5	C	keyboard
	→ Exercise #2	6	D	without
		7	D	~~the~~
		8	D	the sun
		9	A	~~it~~
		10	C	~~be~~ are
		11	A	~~am~~
		12	D	lives/lived
		13	C	laptop
		14	D	~~is~~
		15	A	~~it~~
		16	B	are coming
		17	B	~~the~~
		18	B	staff
		19	B	Canadians
		20	B	suspected
		21	D	or not
		22	B	it off
108	Vocabulary	1	B	
	→ Exercise #2	2	B	
		3	B	
		4	D	
		5	C	
		6	D	
		7	D	
		8	B	
		9	B	
		10	B	
		11	A	
		12	A	
		13	C	
		14	D	
		15	A	
		16	C	
		17	A	
		18	D	

PG.	TASK	?#	ANSWERS	
109	Structure	1	C	
	→ Exercise #3	2	D	
		3	B	
		4	C	
		5	B	
		6	B	
		7	A	
		8	B	
		9	C	
		10	B	
		11	C	
		12	D	
				CORRECTIONS
111	Written Expression	1	C	been having
	→ Exercise #3	2	D	there are
		3	C	testing purposes
		4	B	therefore, it is not possible
		5	B	courses
		6	C	whole
		7	D	proficiency
		8	D	argument
		9	C	into the cup
		10	D	and summarizing arguments
		11	B	with examples
		12	A	that/which designs
		13	B	a better place
		14	A	you focus on…
113	Vocabulary	1	A	
	→ Exercise #3	2	C	
		3	A	
		4	C	
		5	D	
		6	C	
		7	D	
		8	D	
		9	B	
		10	B	
		11	B	
		12	D	
		13	C	

PG.	TASK	?#	ANSWERS	
113	Vocabulary (cont'd)	14	A	
	→ Exercise #3	15	A	
		16	A	
		17	A	
		18	B	

PG.	TASK	?#	ANSWERS	
114	Structure	1	C	
	→ Exercise #4	2	A	
		3	D	
		4	A	
		5	C	
		6	A	
		7	D	
		8	B	
		9	C	
		10	A	
		11	A	
		12	C	
		13	D	
		14	B	
		15	A	
		16	B	
		17	B	
		18	A	
				CORRECTIONS
117	Written Expression	1	C	it
	→ Exercise #4	2	B	school's
		3	B	the new policy
		4	A	Animal behavior
		5	A	Next are
		6	C	literary character
		7	D	with an adverbial clause
		8	C	non-fiction
		9	D	natural gas
		10	B	eating insects
		11	A	rising off/rising off of/rising from
		12	A	was fought
		13	C	less developed nations
		14	B	student's

PG.	TASK	?#	ANSWERS	
119	Vocabulary	1	C	
	→ Exercise #4	2	D	
		3	A	
		4	A	
		5	D	
		6	B	
		7	D	
		8	A	
		9	C	
		10	D	
		11	A	
		12	A	
		13	A	
		14	C	
		15	A	
		16	B	
		17	D	
		18	D	

PG.	TASK	?#	ANSWERS	
120	Structure	1	B	
	→ Exercise #5	2	C	
		3	D	
		4	A	
		5	B	
		6	D	
		7	B	
		8	B	
		9	C	
		10	A	
		11	D	
		12	A	
				CORRECTIONS
122	Written Expression	1	D	more ~~than~~
	→ Exercise #5	2	B	Germany
		3	D	perfectly ripened
		4	D	mountain
		5	A	Many archeologists
		6	A	Desert
		7	B	an organism's
		8	A	include

PG.	TASK	?#	ANSWERS	CORRECTIONS
122	Written Expression (cont'd)	9	D	animal's life
	→ Exercise #5	10	B	of the
		11	D	consumed
		12	C	three
124	Vocabulary	1	A	
	→ Exercise #5	2	A	
		3	D	
		4	D	
		5	D	
		6	A	
		7	B	
		8	A	
		9	A	
		10	A	
		11	D	
		12	C	
		13	A	
		14	B	
		15	B	
		16	A	
		17	A	
		18	D	

PG.	TASK	?#	ANSWERS	
125	Structure	1	A, D, B	
	→ Exercise #6	2	D, B, C	
		3	B, A, B	
		4	B, A, D	
		5	B, B, A	
		6	D, C, A	
		7	D, C, C	
		8	A, A, A	
		9	B, A, D	
		10	B, C, C	
		11	A, B, C	
		12	B, D, D	
				CORRECTIONS
128	Written Expression	1	D	space architect
	→ Exercise #6	2	D	penalized
		3	A	Analyze the

PG.	TASK	?#	ANSWERS	CORRECTIONS
128	Written Expression (cont'd)	4	C	whose mother
	→ Exercise #6	5	A	were part of
		6	D	numerical data
		7	D	neighboring tribe
		8	C	Australia
		9	C	as do
		10	A	documentary filmmaker
		11	C	to identify
		12	C	make a
131	Vocabulary	1	C	
	→ Exercise #6	2	A	
		3	A	
		4	B	
		5	B	
		6	A	
		7	A	
		8	A	
		9	A	
		10	A	
		11	C	
		12	A	
		13	D	
		14	C	
		15	C	
		16	B	
		17	B	
		18	D	

PG.	TASK	?#	ANSWERS	
132	Structure	1	C, D, D	
	→ Exercise #7	2	C, A, B	
		3	C, A, D	
		4	D, C, A	
		5	A, C, A	
		6	D, B, C	
		7	C, A, C	
		8	B, A, C	
		9	D, A, A	
		10	C, A, B	

PG.	TASK	?#	ANSWERS	
132	Structure (cont'd)	11	A, A, B	
	→ Exercise #7	12	B, D, A	
				CORRECTIONS
135	Written Expression	1	A	a. passages
	→ Exercise #7		B	b. in a book
		2	B	b. ~~he~~
			D	d. package it
		3	A	a. throughout
			C	c. similarities
		4	A	a. feel
			B	b. Worse
		5	A	a. short stories
			D	d. will be
		6	B	b. differently
			C	c. practicing
		7	A	a. philosopher
			B	b. essentially
		8	A	a. corrupt
			D	d. each other
		9	C	c. their way
			D	d. scholars
		10	A	a. found in
			B	b. reach up to
		11	B	b. nor a planet
			D	d. with
		12	A	a. ~~it~~
			D	d. of it
138	Vocabulary	1	A	
	→ Exercise #7	2	C	
		3	A	
		4	C	
		5	D	
		6	C	
		7	B	
		8	A	
		9	B	
		10	A	
		11	A	
		12	C	
		13	A	

PG.	TASK	?#	ANSWERS	
138	Vocabulary (cont'd)	14	B	
	→ Exercise #7	15	D	
		16	A	
		17	B	
		18	C	

PG.	TASK	?#	ANSWERS	
139	Structure	1	A, D, B, A	
	→ Exercise #8	2	B, B, D, A	
		3	D, B, A, D	
		4	D, A, A, B	
		5	B, B, A, A	
		6	C, C, C, A	
		7	A, C, B, A	
		8	B, D, A, B	
		9	A, C, D, A	
		10	C, B, D, D	
		11	B, A, D, A	
		12	B, A, C, B	
				CORRECTIONS
144	Written Expression	1	A	a. carnivorous
	→ Exercise #8		B	b. which feeds
			E	e. label
		2	A	a. More specifically
			B	b. at an
			E	c. on a fixed
		3	B	b. dates from
			C	c. proceed
			D	d. might be
		4	A	a. used a
			B	b. unable to
			D	d. by which
		5	B	b. do
			D	d. the most
			E	e. dangerous
		6	A	a. We've been
			C	b. quite the
			E	e. whereas
		7	A	a. empire
			B	b. 4,200
			E	e. came

PG.	TASK	?#	ANSWERS	CORRECTIONS
144	Written Expression (cont'd) → Exercise #8	8	A C D	a. outlines c. goals d. research is
		9	A B D	a. compile b. so vast d. ~~they~~
		10	B D E	b. dawn of d. tree bark e. today's
148	Vocabulary	1	A	
	→ Exercise #8	2	D	
		3	B	
		4	D	
		5	B	
		6	D	
		7	A	
		8	A	
		9	B	
		10	A	
		11	A	
		12	B	
		13	B	
		14	D	
		15	A	
		16	A	
		17	B	
		18	A	

PG.	TASK	?#	ANSWERS
149	Structure	1	B, A, D, B
	→ Exercise #9	2	A, D, B, C
		3	B, C, B, D
		4	D, A, D, D
		5	B, B, B, A
		6	A, D, A, B
		7	C, A, D, A
		8	D, A, D, B
		9	C, A, B, A
		10	B, B, B, A

PG.	TASK	?#	ANSWERS	CORRECTIONS
152	Written Expression → Exercise #9	1	A B E	a. an argument b. philosophy e. to buy
		2	A B E	a. America b. freed from e. a fascist
		3	C D E	c. married d. ~~they~~ e. clues
		4	A B C	a. illicit alcohol b. ~~Albeit~~, Also/In addition c. luck ran out
		5	A B C	a. ~~as a result~~ because it has b. controlled environment c. the role of
		6	A B D	a. profiling b ~~be~~, to determine d. entered into
		7	A D E	a. lacked punctuation d. rejected e. The rise of
		8	B D E	b. ~~people~~, or more buffalo d. lined up on e. ~~it~~, hunting is
		9	A C E	a. was asked c. banana leaf e. testament
		10	B C D	b. job ladder c. ~~similarly~~, in contrast/however d. on the job ladder
156	Vocabulary → Exercise #9	1	B	
		2	D	
		3	A	
		4	B	
		5	A	
		6	A	
		7	C	
		8	B	

PG.	TASK	?#	ANSWERS	
156	Vocabulary (cont'd)	9	D	
	→ Exercise #9	10	C	
		11	A	
		12	A	
		13	C	
		14	B	
		15	A	
		16	A	
		17	A	
		18	A	

PG.	TASK	?#	ANSWERS	
157	Structure	1	C, A, A, D	
	→ Exercise #10	2	C, B, C, A	
		3	B, A, C, B	
		4	D, A, D, B	
		5	D, C, C, C	
		6	C, A, A, D	
		7	C, A, D, A	
		8	B, C, A, A	
		9	C, A, D, D	
		10	C, C, A, A	
				CORRECTIONS
160	Written Expression → Exercise #10	1	C D E F	c. cancerous cells d. cells affected e. the patient's f. side effects
		2	A B C F	a. Canada b. strips of c. it's small size f. cone-shaped
		3	A C D E	a. transformative c. strike-slip quake d. separates e. on the ocean floor
		4	A D E F	a. in the world d. most coveted e. ascending Everest f. to live at the
		5	B	b. sunlight

PG.	TASK	?#	ANSWERS	CORRECTIONS
160	Written Expression (cont'd) → Exercise #10	5	D E F	d. which need e. do not cut down f. eco-friendly
		6	A B C F	a. which has found b. ~~the~~ c. wildlife f. mice
		7	B C D F	b. food gathering c. also found in d. ~~the~~ f. quite well
		8	A C D E	a. organisms b. to generate d. occurs e. germinated
		9	A B C D	a. rivalry b. survival c. a constant supply d. which their
		10	A B D F	a. women b. practical d. on top of that f. Turkish pantaloons
165	Vocabulary	1	D	
	→ Exercise #10	2	D	
		3	C	
		4	B	
		5	A	
		6	B	
		7	C	
		8	C	
		9	D	
		10	D	
		11	A	
		12	D	
		13	C	
		14	B	
		15	A	
		16	A	
		17	A	
		18	A	

TOEFL vs. IELTS Conversion Charts

TOEFL Score	IELTS Band
0–31	0–4
32–34	4.5
35–45	5
46–59	5.5
60–78	6
79–93	6.5
94–101	7
102–109	7.5
110-114	8
115-117	8.5
118–120	9

TOEFL Reading	IELTS Reading	TOEFL Listening	IELTS Listening
0–2	0–4	0–2	0–4
3	4.5	3	4.5
4–7	5	4–6	5
8-12	5.5	7-11	5.5
13–18	6	12-19	6
19-23	6.5	20-23	6.5
24–26	7	24–26	7
27-28	7.5	27	7.5
29	8	28	8
29	8.5	29	8.5
30	9	30	9

TOEFL Speaking	IELTS Speaking	TOEFL Writing	IELTS Writing
0-11	0–4	0-11	0–4
12-13	4.5	12-13	4.5
14-15	5	14-17	5
16-17	5.5	18-20	5.5
18-19	6	21-23	6
20-22	6.5	24-26	6.5
23	7	27-28	7
24-25	7.5	29	7.5
26-27	8	30	8
28-29	8.5	30	8.5
30	9	30	9

Notes